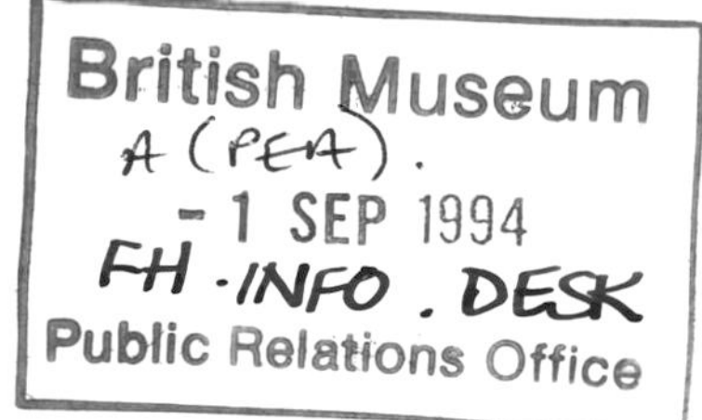

Museums and children with learning difficulties

THE BIG FOOT

Museums and children with learning difficulties

THE BIG FOOT

Anne Pearson
Chitra Aloysius

Published for the Trustees of the British Museum by
British Museum Press

The Trustees of the British Museum gratefully acknowledge the support of the following sponsors, who made this project possible:

The Office of Arts and Libraries (now the Department of National Heritage)
The Calouste Gulbenkian Foundation
The Prudential Corporation
The British Museum Society
The British Council

Published by British Museum Press
A division of British Museum Publications
46 Bloomsbury Street, London WC1B 3QQ

A catalogue record for this book is available from the British Library.

ISBN 0 7141 1744 7

Designed by John Hawkins
Typeset by Create
Printed in Great Britain by The Bath Press

Front cover: An enormous marble foot made in the second century AD and found at Alexandria in Egypt. It may come from a seated statue of the Egyptian god Serapis which, when complete, would have been over 60 feet high. This sculpture proved to be the favourite object used in the British Museum project.

Back cover: A group of children from Beckton School in the London borough of Newham admire the 'big foot'. Clockwise from left: Viki, Tiku, Helen, Kevin, Danny, Tas and Abdul.

The Authors

Anne Pearson is a member of the British Museum Education Service and a regular contributor to the public lecture programme. She is a founder member of the Museums and Galleries Disability Association and author of several books for children and schools on the ancient world.

Chitra Aloysius has been for 23 years a teacher in special education. Following a BA in History of Art, she completed an MA on 'Art Galleries and Special Schools' in 1990. Visits to museums and galleries have become an integral part of her work with children with moderate and severe learning difficulties.

Contents

Preface

by Hazel Moffat HMI

This publication makes a valuable contribution to an area of museum education which has so far been given little prominence. In concentrating on children with learning difficulties it highlights ways in which museum resources can be an exciting and powerful stimulus for their studies and personal development.

The project on which the book focuses owes much to the innovative approach of the two authors and the willing support of the teachers whose pupils visited the British Museum. Above all the children are to be congratulated on the quality of their work. Their responses showed that with careful preparation, a clearly defined task and access to inspiring artefacts, they could become engrossed, begin to develop an awareness of past societies and use various media to record their impressions.

The outcome was sometimes well beyond the expected level of achievement. At the same time the project shows the barriers to learning that can exist in museums for children with learning difficulties. Ways of overcoming them can be of benefit to all museum visitors.

The main project was preceded and followed by seminars at the British Museum which helped to share examples of good work undertaken at the museum and elsewhere in England and the United States of America. Some of this work and more recent examples of learning strategies are also outlined. All of this should help to continue the process of sharing and encourage others to develop museum-based projects for children with learning difficulties.

Many people in Great Britain and abroad will find this book of interest. Museum staff, teachers in mainstream and special schools, advisers and teacher trainers could explore how the approaches described here could be used more widely. In this way, education in museums will be experienced by more children and enrich the lives of those for whom learning is a particular challenge.

ACKNOWLEDGEMENTS

The authors express their grateful thanks to all those who made the project possible, first to the children themselves and their parents and teachers. Many thanks are also due to other advisers and consultants who gave their valuable advice and assistance, in particular Renee Wells, Hazel Moffat and Carolyn Keen.

The authors also wish to thank all the members of the British Museum Education Service for their help with the project and with this book. Particular thanks go to John Reeve, Penny Bateman and Patsy Vanags for their valuable advice and assistance.

CHAPTER ONE

Museums and children with learning difficulties

There are no limits to the age, origin and objectives of those who can derive educational benefits from visiting the Museum. The Education Service aims to make the Museum more accessible for specific groups by providing advice, teaching and materials, as well as contributing in various ways to a better experience for all visitors.

The above may be described as the mission statement of the British Museum Education Service for 1993/94 and it underpins the aims and intentions of the work outlined in this book. This work concentrates on the use of museum collections by children with learning difficulties. Although it is concerned mainly with the British Museum, examples of educational initiatives with children at other museums and galleries, both in Britain and America, are described in Chapters 5 and 6.

DEFINITIONS

The term 'learning difficulties' comes under the umbrella definition 'special needs', which has been in general use in Britain since the 1974–78 Warnock Committee of Inquiry into Special Education which led to the 1981 Education Act on Special Needs. The term refers to children with physical and/or sensory disabilities and those with learning difficulties. The history of special education is described in Chapter 2 of the Warnock Report:

Special education for the handicapped in Great Britain is of relatively recent origin. The very first schools for the blind and deaf were founded in the lifetime of Mozart; those for the physically handicapped awaited the Great Exhibition; day schools for the mentally handicapped and the epileptic arrived with the motorcar; whilst special provision for the delicate, maladjusted and speech impaired children is younger than living memory.[1]

The work described in this book is founded on a number of established principles relating to the education of children with special needs. They are as follows:

Special educational needs are no longer seen as caused solely by factors within the child. They are recognised as the outcome of the interaction between the strengths and weaknesses of the child and the resources and deficiencies of the child's environment. It is therefore not meaningful or even possible to draw a clear dividing line which separates the 'handicapped' from the 'non-handicapped'.

All children are entitled to education. The aims of education are the same for all children, but the means by which the aims can be achieved differ, as does the extent to which they may be achieved.

All schools have a responsibility to identify and meet children's special educational needs, and all children should be educated with their peers as long as their needs can be met, and it is practicable to do so.[2]

Children are often described as having mild, moderate or severe learning difficulties. Children with mild learning difficulty have needs which might be met by an ordinary school. Those with moderate learning difficulties have needs which sometimes need to be met in a special school or in a mainstream school with extra support. Children with severe learning difficulties usually attend special schools.

There are also children with specific learning difficulties, a category which includes dyslexia. This is defined as a syndrome, a cluster of problems with short term working memory, especially speech and verbal memory. Its effects include difficulties with literacy and numeracy to varying degrees. About 2 to 4 per cent of people in the UK are dyslexic.

These definitions can be helpful as describing broad categories of learning needs, but they are rarely helpful or accurate as a description of any individual child. Most children have a broad range of strengths and weaknesses when it comes to their ability to learn and they should therefore always be assessed as individuals. They have the same rights and basic human needs as others and are entitled to the same range of education and training as their contemporaries.

Work in museums with children with learning difficulties bears out the prevailing view that learning difficulty is not a clearly definable and static condition, but rather a continuum. A child who has serious difficulty with words and logical understanding may be capable of a powerful and creative aesthetic response to museum objects and have a marked ability to draw, paint or engage in another activity, such as dance or mime.

Since the 1981 Education Act on Children with Special Needs, a system of identifying certain children with learning difficulties who are covered by a statement detailing their educational requirements has been in operation. Local education authorities (LEAs) have a clearly defined responsibility for these children, but they account for only 2 or 3 per cent of a much larger number of pupils who have special needs.

The 1981 Education Act ... gave expression in legislative terms to a good deal of 'the spirit of Warnock', accepting the basic philosophy, introducing new definitions, imposing new duties on local authorities and schools and providing new safeguards for the rights of parents and children. But (in marked contrast to the United States Federal Government's Public Law 94–142) it carried no commitment by central government to provide substantial additional resources to promote and facilitate change.[3]

As more and more children with special needs are integrated into mainstream schools, teachers will need correspondingly more assistance in teaching the thousands of children who fall outside the statementing system.

RECENT LEGISLATION RELATING TO SPECIAL EDUCATIONAL NEEDS

The Warnock Report (1978):
Report of the Committee of Enquiry into the Education of Handicapped Children and Young People
This ranges widely over the subject and is the result of four years' work by a large committee composed of members from education, health, social services and parent organisations.

One of its important findings was that the process of putting children in categories according to the degree of handicap was counter-productive. Instead, the Committee defined the concept of describing the special educational needs of each individual child. However, the Committee did also recognise that there was a need to retain some descriptive terms for groups of children with learning difficulties.

The 1981 Act on Children with Special Educational Needs
This law was important because it represented a departure from a categorising concept of handicap towards one of special educational need. A system known as statementing was established. Each LEA was required to make statements setting out the special educational needs of individual children within the authority and the arrangements to be made to meet them. These statements were to be maintained and renewed regularly, and access to them by parents was guaranteed.

This Act has been criticised on the basis that it has failed to implement the recommendations of the Warnock Report. No extra resources were allocated to make provision for children with special needs.

1988 Education Reform Act
This Act aimed to raise the expectations of all pupils, including those with statements. It was intended to ensure that these expectations are appropriate so that all children, including those with special educational needs, can benefit to the best of their ability.

Under the legislation the National Curriculum is deemed to be for the use of all registered pupils of compulsory school age including pupils with special educational needs.

The 1992 Education Bill

This Bill is based on the White Paper *Choice and Diversity: A New Framework for Schools*. Part 111 of the Bill is devoted to children with special educational needs and is mainly concerned with statementing and appeal procedures and the future of special schools. It is to a great extent an update of the 1981 Act.

DISABILITY, VISITORS AND MUSEUMS

The field of special education is too often regarded as an optional extra to educational planning.

Most museums in Britain have responded slowly to the needs of children with learning difficulties. Few of them have education staff who are qualified or experienced in special education. Many museums have no education service at all, and where these do exist, they are invariably overstretched to deal with the needs of mainstream schoolchildren and/or adults. Sporadic initiatives have been taken at a wide variety of museums, usually in response to requests from special schools, but this work has rarely been documented and published and therefore remains largely unsung and unevaluated.

What has been achieved has usually been the result of co-operation between individual teachers, curators and educators who have adapted existing resources and facilities to the needs of a particular group of children with special needs.

Museum services for children with learning difficulties are at roughly the same point that museums services for disabled people in general had reached when the Attenborough Report *Arts and Disabled People* was published in 1985. That report drew attention to initiatives in a range of museums and commented:

Valuable as they are, however, such initiatives all too often depend on the enthusiasm of a few individuals, when what is needed is an integrated plan of development in which all the staff are involved. In the result, provision for disabled people remains very patchy even within particular establishments, let alone the country as a whole.[4]

Since 1985, however, museum services for people with physical and sensory disabilities have made some progress. Eilean Hooper-Greenhill, in her book *Museum and Gallery Education*, writes:

By the end of the 1980s, therefore, a considerable amount has been achieved, partly through self-help, but partly also through help from the Carnegie UK Trust and the Museums Galleries Commission. The Royal National Institute for the Blind has also begun to play a stronger role, with its Arts and Leisure Department acting as a catalyst between blind groups and museums. As a result, interest in and provision for visual impairment has, as we have seen, blossomed. Similar growth is required in provision for people with other impairments.[5]

The general lack of arts and educational provision for disabled people ties in with the lack of employment rights for disabled people in the UK and is also a consequence of equal opportunities policies which have no real bite. The legal employment quota of 3 per cent is a quite inadequate reflection of the number of disabled people in the population. A Civil Rights Bill designed to end discrimination against disabled people failed during 1991. A recent publication on *Disabled People and the Visual Arts* states:

It has been suggested that of the half million employees in the subsidised art sector, only 100 are disabled. (Lord Rix, addressing Arts Council/Department of Employment seminar on Employment in the Arts for Disabled People, Brixton 1992.)

Equal Opportunities policies in arts organisations are frequently drawn up by an external body, then set in stone and ticked off as a credit towards fulfilling funding criteria. Instead they should be working documents, fluid in nature, permeating every level of an organisation's structure and practice, constantly reviewed and revised, and urging compulsory rather than casual compliance.[6]

BACKGROUND TO THE BRITISH MUSEUM PROJECT

The legislation which has followed the Warnock Report reflects the changing social attitudes to learning disabilities and the various attempts to improve facilities for the children concerned. The lack of provision in one particular area, museum education, has inspired this publication. One of the authors, Chitra Aloysius, has worked as a teacher in special education since 1970, latterly as creative arts co-ordinator at Beckton school in the London Borough of Newham. Following a BA in the History of Art, she completed an MA on Art Galleries and Special Schools in 1990 at the University of East London.

During visits to art galleries and museums she encountered many groups of mainstream pupils. As a teacher from a special school she was struck by the absence of children with learning difficulties. Convinced that her pupils too should have the opportunity to experience art collections, she began a three year research programme in 1987 to produce evidence to support her view that such children would benefit from museum and gallery education.

Critical Awareness

Chitra believes that by a critical awareness of art children can gain confidence in formulating and expressing views on painting and sculpture. In the world of art they may blossom, rising above the sense of failure and frustration induced by their less successful performance in other basic skills.

Writing in 1993 she explains:

Since Broca discovered in the last century that the speech centre is situated in the left hemisphere, evidence has slowly accumulated to show differences in function between the two sides of the brain. Present researchers use both objective examination of the brain – for example the monitoring of the increased blood supply to the areas involved in specific activities, such as reading aloud – and also subjective responses, as with 'split-brain' patients, where the two halves of the brain have been surgically separated.

Such research may have importance for children with learning difficulties, and also for the teaching of art and design. It is generally accepted that the left hemisphere operates in a logical, analytical and sequential mode, and deals with words and numbers; while the right has a more intuitive, holistic and creative approach, and is better able to appreciate form and space.

The two hemispheres work together, with messages constantly flashing between them. The left hemisphere is normally dominant, but it seems likely that the artist at work makes more use of the right hemisphere, having learnt unconsciously to inhibit the left. Some children with learning difficulties may have an impaired left hemisphere which co-exists with a relatively normal right hemisphere. They may possess a creative faculty that is simply waiting to be awakened. Critical awareness in art programmes may provide a means of reaching untapped areas of the brain.[7]

Beckton Art Club

As there was no formal provision for art and no resources for museum and gallery visiting, Chitra began a lunch-time art club at Hatton School in Redbridge, for children with moderate learning difficulties. This was linked to visits to the National and the Tate Galleries in London.

The aims of the art club were to increase the children's sensitivity to their own world and their capacity for enjoyment and to bridge the gap between the past depicted by the artist and the present experienced by the child. The visit to the galleries meant that 'high art' was made accessible to the children so that they could recognise and appreciate the land and seascapes of Turner, the impressionist paintings of Monet and Seurat, the abstract paintings of Pollock and Matisse, and the expressionist works of Munch.

The key to a successful gallery visit was good classroom preparation spread over several weeks. Each child expressed an opinion on some aspect of a painting, followed by a general discussion in a happy, relaxed atmosphere. Most children wanted to draw and paint during the session, and many came on other days during their playtime to do this. Enough money was raised by one group to cover the cost of the visit to the Tate by the sale of an oil painting created by the group during its final session.

At the Tate a member of the Education staff gave the children a gallery talk, which she extended from half an hour to an hour to allow time to answer the children's questions and comments on works they had not seen before.

Chitra took a group of children with severe learning difficulties from Beckton School to the Monet exhibition at the Royal Academy in December 1990. The children came from various social and ethnic backgrounds and had problems which affected

The Water-Lily Pond, Claude Monet (1840–1926), National Gallery, London.

their speech, concentration and behaviour. The weeks of preparation in the art club enabled them to recognise and enjoy Monet's series of paintings such as *The Poplars*, which show the same scene painted at different times of the day and year. The children appreciated the changing patterns of light and colour, and later, at the Art Club, recaptured the Monet experience by creating designs using the artist's characteristic colours.

The following are examples of the verbal responses of some of the children to the paintings.

Jamie, a child with moderate learning difficulties and behavioural problems who has poor concentration and struggles to write his own name said, 'When I look at paintings it makes me think of other artists and feel like them. I don't just draw. I think how to draw and want to do better, and this makes me happy'.

Laura, who also has moderate learning difficulties, discussed Renoir's *The Umbrellas*: 'His touches of blue get into me, Miss, as if he looked at all those people through a blue cloud'.

The working relationship between Chitra Aloysius and Anne Pearson of the British Museum Education Service (BMES) began at the Monet exhibition. Anne had heard of Chitra's work and made contact with her. At the exhibition with the group she was able to observe at first hand the children's powerful reaction to the paintings. The decision was then made to work together on planning a visit to the British Museum based on similar principles.

THE BRITISH MUSEUM SEMINAR, FEBRUARY 1991

The success of the educational approach at the Tate and other initiatives led several museum educators to consider how best to develop similar learning techniques using their own collections. The BMES had already developed a number of programmes for visitors with disabilities, including two touch exhibitions and a gallery with special touch facilities. It was now particularly interested in extending its services to children with learning difficulties and together with Hazel Moffat, HMI with responsibility for museum education, it held a seminar on the subject in February 1991. This was the first of three seminars concentrating on different aspects of the project as it unfolded.

About forty people (a mixture of museum educators and special needs teachers) participated in an examination of the value of museum learning and how best it can be achieved with children with special needs.

Chitra Aloysius was one of the speakers and described her teaching methods in detail, in particular the strong emphasis on advance planning for the museum visit and the follow-up work which are key elements in her approach.

A number of other practitioners including Carolyn Keen, the then Disability Adviser of the Museums and Galleries Commission, Marilyn Ingle of the Castle

Museum, York, and Isabel Hughes, Hampshire Museums Education Officer, shared experiences and resource ideas relating to visitors with a range of disabilities.

A unique contribution to the day was made by four fifteen- to sixteen-year old students with dyslexia from Mark College in Somerset who gave a presentation of their visits to Taunton Museum and Bristol City Museum and Art Gallery. Using slides they described their experience, clearly outlining how they thought museums could improve design and lay out techniques to enable people with dyslexia to absorb information more easily.

Their contribution provided valuable insights to museum professionals. It was also a remarkable example of self-advocacy by a group of consumers of museum services whose views are not usually heard. (For further details see Chapter 7.)

The Chairman of the Dyslexia Educational Trust, who attended the seminar, emphasised two key points which had clearly emerged: first, that the opinions and criticisms of the children and students with dyslexia should always be essential elements in designing educational provision for them, and, second, that it should always be borne in mind that initiatives which benefit visitors with disabilities invariably enhance the museum experience for everyone.

REFERENCES

1. Warnock Report, *Special Educational Needs* (Cmnd 7212), HMSO, 1978.
2. Daniels, Harry and Ware, Jean (eds), *Special Educational Needs and the National Curriculum: The impact of the Education Reform Act*, Institute of Education, 1991.
3. Adams, Fred (ed.), *Special Education in the 90s*, The Society of Education Officers, Longman Group UK Ltd, 1990.
4. *Arts and Disabled People. The Attenborough Report*, Carnegie United Kingdom Trust, 1985.
5. Hooper-Greenhill, Eilean, *Museums and Gallery Education*, Leicester University Press, 1991
6. Earnscliffe, Jane, *In Through the Front Door, Disabled people and the Visual Arts: Examples of Good Practice*, The Arts Council of Great Britain, 1992.
7. Aloysius, Chitra, 'Art Galleries and Special Schools', *Arts Education*, April 1993.

CHAPTER TWO

The project begins

The interest expressed at the February seminar showed that the work at the National Gallery and elsewhere had struck a chord with many people in museums and education, and that the lack of provision for children with learning difficulties in museums had to be addressed urgently. It was decided to build on this experience and establish a learning difficulties project at the British Museum.

The nature of the collections in the British Museum might be thought to present particular problems in relation to teaching children with learning difficulties. Those areas of the museum traditionally used by mainstream schools are primarily those which relate to the ancient world (such as Egypt, Greece, Rome and early Medieval Britain) and therefore to societies markedly different from those which modern children experience.

It is precisely this difference, this distinct 'otherness' in terms of value systems, religion and daily life, which excites so many children and makes their visit to the British Museum so pleasurable. Could the same be true for children with learning difficulties? If it can be said that they are less critically aware of their own society than other children, how can they comprehend the nature of ancient civilisations and their artefacts? It was this fundamental question that was addressed in the setting up of the project.

AIMS OF THE PROJECT

In the summer of 1991, the following aims for the project were drawn up:

- to encourage the use of museum facilities by children with learning difficulties.
- to enhance the quality of museum education for children with a range of learning difficulties.
- to link museum and gallery visits to the National Curriculum by providing resources and experiences linked to the National Curriculum attainment targets.

- to explore new teaching methods and approaches arising from the impact of British Museum objects on children with severe learning difficulties.
- to introduce to the children a critical awareness of art, building on the experience of earlier work at the National Gallery, the Royal Academy and the Tate Gallery.

This programme was quite ambitious and its realisation depended on a marriage of the skills of both museum education and classroom teaching. The authors therefore set about acquiring funding from various sources to allow for the secondment of Chitra Aloysius to the BMES for the autumn term 1991.

Her role would be, in the words of the application for sponsorship, 'to work with a control group of children with learning difficulties, to develop, evaluate and test ideas emerging from the February seminar. Teaching materials will be written and piloted during this phase'. In this process she would work closely with the staff of the BMES, drawing on their resources and knowledge of the collections.

Two further phases of the project were also planned. There would be a follow-up seminar to discuss and evaluate the teaching materials and visits. The main object of this second seminar would be:

- to produce practical access information for teachers to help them make museum visits with children with learning difficulties.
- to encourage the greater use of museums as exciting, valuable educational resources.

There would also be a publication evaluating the results of the work of the project.

FINDING SPONSORSHIP

The BMES prepared a sponsorship application which described the work in progress and outlined the case for development. The presentation was largely the work of Shelby Mamdani, a special assistant in the Education Service, dealing, among other things, with aspects of sponsorship.

We are grateful to the sponsoring organisations for their generous response to our application for funding. Without them the various elements in the research programme could not have been carried out. (For a list of sponsors see page 4.)

PARTICIPATING SCHOOLS

The schools chosen to take part in the project were selected to reflect the diversity of educational need. The teachers included colleagues and former colleagues of Chitra Aloysius who had already shown an interest in expanding the art curriculum for children with learning difficulties. They were also to some extent self-selecting in that they had to be able to commit themselves to involvement in the project at the appropriate time.

The children had either moderate or severe learning difficulties and their ages ranged from nine to nineteen plus. None of the children were ambulant disabled, but some of them were sensorily impaired, with hearing and vision difficulties.

Their particular learning difficulties varied. The children had a range of needs: moderate learning difficulties, severe learning difficulties, communication difficulties and emotional and behavioural problems. (For the names of the schools and the teachers who participated in the project, see Appendix 1.)

All the schools which took part were from the inner city or close to it, except Arbour Vale School which is in Reading, about fifty miles from London. The children had various ethnic origins and social backgrounds. For a high proportion of the children, English was their second language and none of them had visited the British Museum before. The cost of transport to the Museum for the two visits was covered by the school budgets in all cases.

THE NATIONAL CURRICULUM

All state schools in England now follow a National Curriculum. It is a framework for the school curriculum defined by law, made up of core and other foundation subjects which all pupils must study from five to sixteen years of age. The core subjects are science, mathematics and English and the other foundation subjects are technology, geography, history, art, music, physical education and modern foreign languages.

Like other museum education services, the BMES has been profoundly affected by the introduction of the National Curriculum, especially in history. The Museum played a part in the selection of the subjects chosen and its collections are relevant for many of the Key Stage 2 topics.

Special needs teachers assess pupils in line with national standards in order to prevent them from being isolated from the rest of the education system. They are doing this creatively in ways which make the National Curriculum requirements for mainstream children accessible for their children.

All the participating teacher/co-ordinators wanted to integrate the museum project into their classroom teaching and the requirements of Key Stages 1 and 2 of the National Curriculum. (In mainstream schools Key stage 1 covers five to seven year-olds and Key Stage 2 is the seven to eleven age group).

The National Curriculum subject areas which were covered by the BM project were science, mathematics, English, technology, history and art.

Within the National Curriculum subjects are split into smaller topics and Attainment Targets (ATs) are set, involving the acquiring of specific skills. The ATs selected by the project co-ordinators were chosen to suit the particular abilities of their pupils.

There are ten levels of achievement for each AT in most subjects. A mainstream child might be expected to reach level two or three on the scale by the age of seven. Pupils with special educational needs might well take longer to reach the same level, but can still be working towards the same targets at their own speed and ability.

An example of such parallel activity can be seen clearly in the art curriculum. In exploring and appreciating a particular colour, perhaps blue, one child might use fine brushwork and concentrate on detail and shade, while a child with severe learning difficulties might experience the same colour using finger paint and exploring texture and patterns.

Some of the most interesting educational work inspired by the National Curriculum is in fact being undertaken by special needs teachers who are adapting the curriculum to the needs of their pupils. It has been found, for example, that the floating and sinking test in science, where children have to place different objects in water, has been popular with special needs children.

It might appear paradoxical that teachers of children with learning difficulties are exploring ways of introducing investigative and problem-solving activities when recent reports are promoting a more structured approach in primary schools. However what has become apparent is the value of collaboration between special education teachers and subject advisory teachers in producing activities and approaches that develop skills which allow children to experience a full curriculum.[1]

APPLICATION OF THE NATIONAL CURRICULUM TO THE BRITISH MUSEUM PROJECT

The British Museum project is thus part of a wider exploratory process in the education of children with learning difficulties which concentrates on practical and aesthetic activity rather than verbal and analytical skills.

The project co-ordinators hoped that the museum experience would foster skills of observation, concentration and hand-eye co-ordination. Drawing museum objects in the galleries and other forms of art work were perceived to be key elements of this. Gallery work with two- and three-dimensional objects would enhance an awareness of spatial relationships and begin to develop in the children some awareness of past societies.

Once in the museum, communicating with education, security and other staff might help the children to develop social skills through speaking and listening and articulating personal preferences. The public and sometimes crowded nature of the BM galleries where the children would be working might also engender other social skills, such as taking turns and interacting with other visitors.

CHOOSING THE GALLERIES

The choice of galleries used in the project reflected the various ideas and instincts of the teachers and museum staff involved about what would be most likely to work with these particular children.

The requirements of the National Curriculum were also looked at in relation to certain objects and categories of objects. The subject areas chosen were the Greeks, the Egyptians, the Assyrians, the Vikings, Roman mosaics and Roman sculpture.

Choices were also based on the long experience of the BMES in arranging visits for huge numbers (*c*.130,000 per annum) of primary schoolchildren. There was plenty of educational material already available to help the teachers in planning their work programme.

The entrance to the Nimrud gallery, British Museum, flanked by a human-headed lion and bull.

Brief descriptions of the galleries chosen for the project and their contents are given in Chapter 3.

THE TEACHER/CO-ORDINATORS

The teacher/co-ordinators came to the Museum for a preparatory visit and discussion. They used the BMES library and the educational resources which were already in existence for use by primary and secondary schools. (For the list of resources used see Appendix 4.)

Thorough preparation for a museum visit is regarded as standard practice in the teaching profession, but in the case of children with learning difficulties it takes on even greater importance. Since many of these children have poor concentration it is vital they arrive so well prepared that they greet the exhibits as old friends and thereby gain the maximum benefit from the visit.

All the teacher/co-ordinators, with the help of Chitra Aloysius and the BMES advice and resources, devised their own methods of preparation to suit the children, using the National Curriculum as a guide.

The pattern of the project was to be as follows:

- classroom preparation
- the visit itself
- classroom discussion after the visit
- practical work after the visit.

REFERENCES

1. Robbins, Brian, 'No easy option', *Junior Education*, April 1991.

NOTE

The National Curriculum for England and Wales is under review as this book goes to press. Details of National Curriculum requirements quoted in this chapter and in the following pages are, of course, those in force at the time of the project.

CHAPTER THREE

And so to the British Museum

This chapter concentrates on four of the six groups of children in the project. Their work clearly represents different levels of ability, teaching techniques and approaches to gallery activities.

The schools involved were Castle School in the Greek galleries, Beckton School in the Egyptian galleries, Gurney School in the Roman mosaics galleries and Hylesford School in the Wolfson gallery of Roman sculpture. None of these schools had ever visited the British Museum before.

Two other groups of children from John F. Kennedy School, Newham and Abbevale School, Slough worked in the Assyrian Gallery and the Early Medieval Gallery and a description of these visits is included at the end of the chapter.

THE GREEK GALLERIES

Ten children from Castle school, aged eight to fourteen, took part in a study of the ancient Greeks. The children had a range of special needs which included moderate learning difficulty as well as communication, emotional and behavioural difficulties.

Their teacher/co-ordinator, Marion Price, had decided to focus on Greek home life as a theme, in line with classroom studies on the subject already selected for the term. As she was uncertain as to how the children would respond to an ancient culture, she hoped to capture their interest by approaching the subject through familiar topics such as eating and drinking.

In advance of the museum visit, the children were shown postcards and slides, mainly scenes of daily life from Greek vases. This gave them an initial insight not only into the scenes portrayed, but also into the shape and general appearance of Greek pottery.

They were taught how to make pottery inspired by Greek vase shapes, and also engaged in written and art work on Greek subjects. This meant that when they arrived at the Museum and were passing through Greek Room 3, they were able to recognise

Castle school pupil working in the ground-floor Greek gallery.

(*Right*) The Sophilos bowl, a Greek black-figure vase, and (*above*) the child's drawing.

(*Right*) Greek black-figure amphora. (*Below*) Child's drawing of the amphora, and other drawings inspired by Greek vases.

Marble frieze from Xanthus in Lycia, on display in the lower Greek gallery.

objects of ancient Greek manufacture without difficulty and respond to them, which they did with delight. (This gallery contains Greek art from about 1100 BC to about 520 BC and has stone sculpture, bronze and terracotta figurines, vases and jewellery.)

The group then moved on to Greek Room 5 where they were encouraged to wander, observe and discuss the objects with their teacher and two other helpers. (Greek Room 5 has red figure vases, bronzes and terracottas from *c*.500 BC to 440 BC.)

The children were then asked to choose their favourite object as a subject for drawing. In this way they were able to exercise freedom of choice and decision-making skills in line with the National Curriculum targets.

While they were drawing they seemed oblivious of other visitors in the gallery. Some children sat on the floor to draw, while others preferred to stand. One child made an excellent composite miniature drawing using motifs from several different vases. Another, who has a communication disorder, completely ignored the vases and drew instead part of a marble frieze from Xanthus in Lycia, carved with cocks and hens, which is displayed around the walls of the gallery.

The Harpy Tomb

In the centre of Room 5 is the so-called Harpy Tomb. It is dated to 480 BC and also comes from Xanthus. Its marble surfaces are carved with scenes of sitting and standing human figures. There are also winged female creatures, formerly thought to be evil harpies, but now identified as sirens who are gently carrying off the souls of the departed (which look rather like small sleeping children) to the world of the dead.

This object attracted the attention of all the children and produced one of the most successful drawings of the whole Project. The boy who drew it was not interested in

(*Below*) Frieze from the Harpy tomb, lower Greek gallery, and (*above*) child's drawing of it.

the mythical story, but was totally absorbed in the pictorial qualities of the tomb and copied it with skill and flair.

The group then moved on to Greek Room 8 where the classical sculptures from the Parthenon are displayed. This is a very large room, always full of visitors. The sculptures being composed of one medium, white marble, at first glance present less visual variety than the two earlier galleries. However, the children again applied themselves quickly to observational drawing, working carefully and silently and showing distinct reluctance to leave the gallery after half an hour.

Much special needs teaching is highly concentrated and directed by the teacher. One of the values of a museum experience is that it can allow the teacher to operate a more hands-off policy, enabling the children to take the lead and to respond more personally to the challenge. With the Greeks this approach was particularly successful. Marion Price was delighted with the curiosity and commitment displayed by the children, which greatly exceeded her expectations.

They finished off their visit in the Greek and Roman Life Room (69). This room has a range of objects from classical antiquity relating to everyday life. The objects are arranged thematically, e.g. farming and food, the house, the life of women, marriage and funerals, toys and childhood.

A Greek banquet

To celebrate the end of the Greek Project and to share the experience with the rest of Castle School, an end of term Greek banquet was held, which staff and students attended in classical dress. This fitted naturally into the home life theme of their Greek study. The banquet consisted of typical Greek food, including a lentil dish. One of the teachers had researched Greek cookery and found the following ancient Greek recipe.

5th Century BC Greek Recipe

(Enough to feed 80 people)

INGREDIENTS

7lbs of cooked lentils	*fresh oregano*
20 onions	*fresh coriander*
9 teaspoons of salt	*green garum*
½ pint of olive oil	*anchovy essence*
½ pint of sesame oil	

Fry the onions with olive oil and salt. Add cooked lentils and sesame oil and garum. Cook in earthenware pot with lid at fairly high temperature. Sprinkle with fresh herbs. Serve with bread.

THE EGYPTIAN GALLERIES

Beckton School chose the Egyptians as a theme for their museum experience. A group of nine children (aged nine to fourteen) with severe learning difficulties was involved and the project was organised in the school and at the Museum by Chitra Aloysius and the head teacher, Maggie Angele. As in the case of Castle School with the Greeks, the whole of Beckton School 'went Egyptian' for the autumn term. Each class made posters of Egyptian designs and colours which were displayed in the central hall.

The dramatic nature and the sheer quantity of the BM Egyptian collections attracted the staff to the subject of Egypt. The variety of Egyptian decorative motifs and religious symbols was felt to be a rich source of material which would stimulate the children's visual imagination and artistic skill. As these children had belonged to the art club, and had visited the Monet exhibition (see Chapter 1) they already had experience of art at the Royal Academy and the Tate Gallery. The real question was whether they would respond with the same enthusiasm to three dimensional archaeological material as well as they had to pictures.

Ancient hieroglyphs and modern Makaton

Inculcating a sense of the passage of time and the concept of an ancient civilisation is a serious challenge for teachers of children with severe learning difficulties. The culture of ancient Egypt awakened in the children an awareness of the past. An important catalyst in this process proved to be the hieroglyphs.

The pictographic nature of Egyptian writing fascinated the children and was, as a concept, not at all unfamiliar to them because they were already used to working with Makaton symbols (see Appendix 6). They were also used to doing pre-writing patterns and exercises, zigzags, curves, spirals, etc.

During the pre-visit classroom preparation, one of the children's tasks was to write their names in hieroglyphs. They took great pleasure in this activity and at the Museum they sought out, from among the inscribed sarcophagi, the hieroglyphs which most closely corresponded to those which made up their names.

Egyptian hieroglyphs on a Fourth Dynasty limestone tomb relief.

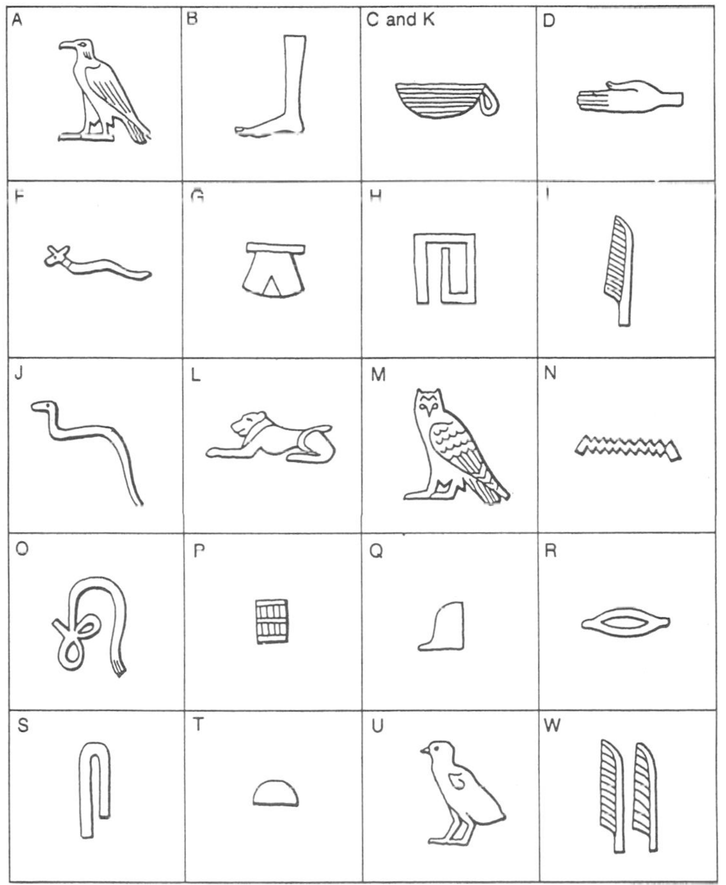

An 'alphabet' of hieroglyphs.

This exploring took place mainly in Room 25, where there is a collection of sculpture from many periods of Egyptian history. The artefacts were mainly produced for temples and tombs in a variety of stone: marble and limestone, granite, sandstone and schist.

The study of the Egyptians was planned to link with a number of National Curriculum core and other foundation subjects which included English, History, Design Technology and Art.

In English they were working to AT 1: Speaking and listening. In discussion sessions about the Egyptians the children's ability to articulate and exchange ideas noticeably improved both at the museum and in school. They learned new sounds and words and expanded their use of Makaton sign language.

Writing their own names in English and hieroglyphs helped with AT 2 and 3, Reading and Writing. Not all the children were able to recognise the words 'Egyptians' and 'British Museum', but they all learnt to say the words using a combination of signs and speech.

In the National Curriculum History unit they were working to AT 1 at levels 1–4. Through their preparation sessions at school and then seeing the objects themselves at the Museum, the children began to be familiar with some of the distinctive characteristics of Egyptian art. They acquired and comprehended words and phrases relating to the passing of time, such as 'old', 'new', 'before', 'after' and 'long ago'.

The ankh and the water-lily.

The ankh and the water-lily

The children were encouraged to find, observe and copy shapes, patterns and symbols used in the decoration of mummy cases and friezes, such as the lotus and the ankh, the symbol of life. Each child was given outline drawings of two Egyptian gods to study and colour.

They recognised certain Egyptian symbols by comparison with modern examples. They responded to the ankh, the Egyptian symbol of life, by making a comparison with the Christian cross.

The natural world, as reflected in Egyptian art, was also meaningful to them. The children loved the water-lilies which frequently feature in Egyptian tomb painting because they also remembered them from the works of Monet whose exhibition they had seen at the Royal Academy (see Chapter 1).

Although the study of such an ancient culture presents particular problems for children with severe learning difficulty, the stimulation of the classroom preparation combined with exposure to real objects gave the children some comprehension of the passage of time and a sense of human continuity. They made comments like, 'The ancient Egyptians liked water-lilies – so do we!'

Kevin studying an Egyptian tomb painting.

Gods and goddesses
In the galleries the children undertook various exercises designed to improve observation, concentration and appreciation. Postcards of distinctive objects were given to them and they were then asked to find the actual object in the gallery. The same method was used in their search for the gods and goddesses which they had studied in class.

They were also invited to choose a subject to draw. Favourite choices were mummy cases, ankh symbols and statues. They tended to choose objects with which they were familiar from classroom preparation. An exception to this was their response to a particularly large and glittering gold mummy case (see colour plate 4). The object had a powerful effect on all of them and they wanted to stay close to it and look at it for a long time.

The children had enough teaching staff with them to receive assistance whenever they wanted it and they spent an uninterrupted hour and a half in the galleries. After lunch there was time to visit the Museum shop and listen to music in an exhibition about Mozart in the British Library. In spite of their learning difficulties and communication problems, these children responded to the Egyptian objects with great excitement and seemed to develop a strong emotional bond with particular objects. They took photographs of each other smiling in front of favourite pieces such as the huge head of Ramses II, 'my friend'.

Integration with Eastlea Community School
An integrated programme linked with the Project involved Beckton students in mainstream Technology classes at nearby Eastlea Community School. Four Beckton students joined a Technology mainstream group of seventeen children at Eastlea to design a wall plaque of Egyptian gods.

The purpose of this was to combine experience, skills and resources. Beckton school could offer their knowledge of Egyptian deities as the subject matter of the plaque, while the children from Eastlea contributed technical competence and their workshop and equipment.

The research and study plans for the plaque were carried out at Beckton school, and the designing and making of the plaque was done at Eastlea. This co-operative venture was undertaken over a period of five weeks with the Beckton students working at Eastlea once a week. The work enabled the students to meet Design Technology AT 1 of the National Curriculum, Identifying needs and opportunities.

AT 2, level 2a of the Design Technology curriculum states, 'use talk, pictures, drawings, models, to develop design proposals, giving simple reasons why they have chosen to make their design'. This task was attempted by the group in their selection of the gods, and in trying to know and understand the appearance and names of the gods and their relationship to the lives of the ancient Egyptians. The children used drawing and colouring to enhance their understanding at this stage.

They met AT 3, Planning and making, in the actual production of the plaque. The children decided that the background of the plaque should represent the sands of Egypt and looked for a wood of the right grain and colour. They selected American redwood as the most appropriate and the figures of the deities were fixed to it.

The actual making of the plaque provided an opportunity to expand the students' vocabulary. New words acquired were 'plywood', 'sandpaper', 'polish', 'fretsaw', 'blade', 'metal', 'steel' and 'goggles'.

Both schools saw the project as an ideal way of integrating pupils with differing abilities. The children from Eastlea worked alongside the Beckton children, happily sharing tools and discussing design problems. Sometimes the Beckton children, as a way of demonstrating that the project had originated with them and was, in a sense, theirs, allocated tasks to the Eastlea children, especially the more tedious ones, like lengthy sandpapering.

The most obvious success of the Project was demonstrated in the harmonious way the children worked together. Behaviour and attitudes to study showed a marked improvement and truancy was almost non-existent during the making of the plaque.

Members of Beckton and Eastlea Schools with their finished plaque.

ROMAN MOSAICS

Roman Africa and Stratford Swimming Pool

Roman mosaics were tackled by Gurney School. Ten children (aged between nine and eleven) with moderate learning difficulties were involved. Their teacher, Cheryl Chant, had selected mosaics as the most accessible category of Roman art for her children. She felt that mosaics, being made up of tiny component parts, would appeal, and the naturalistic animal and bird subject matter would also excite them. She also saw the possibilities of mosaics as an innovative way of teaching concepts of pattern, numbering and design as part of the mathematics, design technology and English elements of the National Curriculum.

As a preliminary exercise, the children were introduced to the concept of mosaic floors at Stratford Swimming Pool. Later they also drew from a mosaic which decorates the local shopping centre in Stratford. They were taught how the mosaics were constructed and helped to appreciate their functional and pictorial value.

On arrival at the Museum the pupils were taken to a large collection of Roman mosaics which are displayed high on the walls flanking a wide staircase. First they completed a brief worksheet (available in the BMES Learning Difficulties Resource Pack). Each child then selected a particular mosaic and settled down to draw. This meant coping with the distracting experience of working on a busy stairway (the main

A group of children drawing Roman mosaics.

The Education Service generally advises against children working around staircases except under the closest supervision.

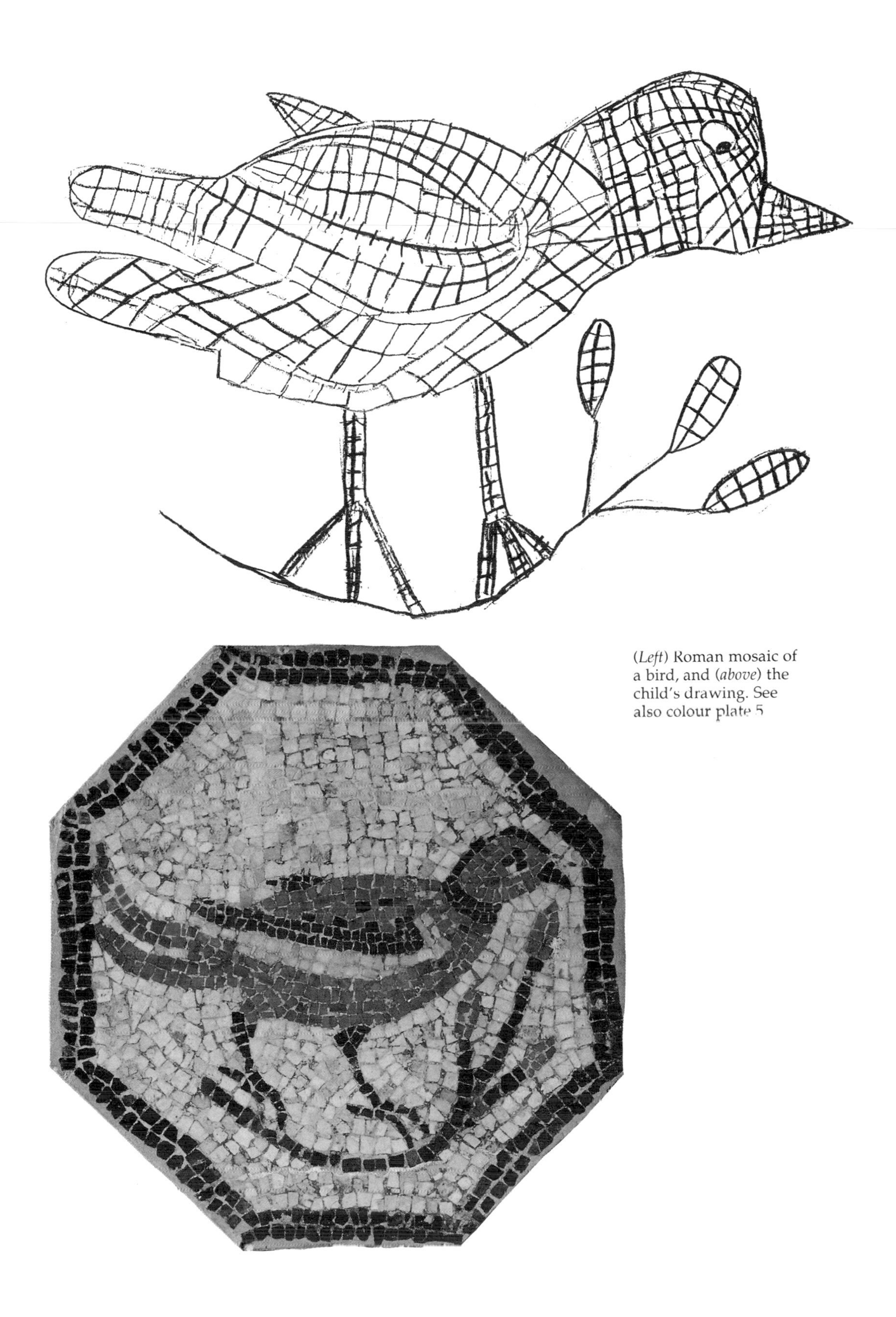

(*Left*) Roman mosaic of a bird, and (*above*) the child's drawing. See also colour plate 5

(*Below*) Roman mosaic of confronted dolphins and (*above*) child's drawing. The child has exaggerated the size of the dolphin's eye.

(*Opposite*) Gurney School children in the Newham Arts Education Centre making their own mosaic.

route up to the Mummy Room) with visitors sometimes blocking the view and interrupting the work in hand. Some found it difficult to concentrate, but others managed well. One boy, absorbed in his mosaic for over an hour, was still completing the background tesserae of his drawing when the others had stopped for lunch.

The children were even more confident on their second visit, nine days later, and soon were absorbed again in their mosaic designs. As a group they concentrated well, not stopping even when other visitors came close and commented on the drawings. After an hour's further work, with a real feeling of achievement among the children, the group made its way to the Upper Egyptian galleries to the mummies, although no formal work was undertaken here. They found the mummies extremely curious and displayed no unease with them.

After that the children went to look at Persian and Indian material. This was deliberately included by the teacher because four members of the group were of Indian origin and one was Iranian. Cheryl wanted the pupils to have a sense of the great scope and variety of the BM collections and also to experience objects from their own cultural background. Although these collections did not form part of this project they clearly have great possibilities for educational use.

Many of the lessons learnt in the galleries were reinforced in classroom work in subsequent weeks. During speech therapy sessions the group recalled their museum visit and discussed mosaics, colours and materials. The speech therapist noticed that

most of the children had understood the purpose of the visit to the Museum. National Curriculum English, AT 1: Speaking and listening levels 2 and 3 were met by the group's discussion sessions, both before and after the museum visits. Each child contributed to the discussion at his or her own level although there was a need for some repetition to consolidate knowledge.

Reading and writing work for the group had to be repetitive and simple. All the children recognised words such as 'British Museum' and 'mosaics' and were involved in copying work. Copying here was used as a teaching method and a way of helping children who had difficulty in forming letters and constructing sentences. The group decided orally what should be recorded. A typical example was, 'We saw the mosaics in the British Museum'. The pupils read out aloud to the class what they had written and in this way museum objects were used as a valuable catalyst in the acquisition of vocabulary.

Tiles and tesserae

As Cheryl had hoped, the mosaics proved to be an excellent way of linking the museum visit with the mathematics curriculum. National Curriculum targets such as matching colours, making a colour chart and the use of sequential numbers from 1 to 30, were tackled. When making their own mosaics the children used numbers as the key to identifying colours, so that they could mix the exact colour later. The group helped to make the ceramic tiles for their own mosaic, rolling out the clay and using mathematical procedures such as measuring, marking and cutting out tiles to a uniform size. Finally they counted the number of tiles necessary to form the components of the final mosaic.

Making observational drawings directly from the mosaics at the Museum gave the children first hand experience of an ancient art form and helped them to meet AT 1, levels 2 and 3 of National Curriculum Art. Their drawings were later used by the children as designs for their own tile and plaster mosaics at Newham Arts Centre. The work of investigation and exploration was developed here where the group worked with Jane Holmes, the advisory teacher, learning how to handle different materials and making their own mosaics. Altogether they had three sessions at the Art Centre. These sessions were organised by the teacher as a way of reinforcing the technical knowledge acquired in the children's study of mosaics.

All the children gained some competence at level 2 using different tools. They worked with pencils, paint, pastels and a variety of textural materials such as pulses, shells, beads and plastics and plaster. They developed their use of line drawings, experimenting with textured materials and patterns. The mosaic patterns, particularly the decorated borders with their repeated motifs, were especially challenging. They were studied, drawn and then developed into the children's own designs on plaster. The project expanded their knowledge of colours and their capacity to distinguish

The Wolfson basement gallery.

between subtle shades. They learnt how to mix colours to acquire a desired match and how to produce tonal effects, and how to appreciate light and dark shades.

The art work produced by the children was of a far higher quality than any they had achieved before. They sustained the high standard in later work, suggesting that the museum experience had inspired them and helped them to improve their artistic skills. One boy in particular continued to use a mosaic format in his own artwork as much as a year later, showing how strongly he had been influenced by the art form.

ROMAN SCULPTURE

The Roman sculpture topic was chosen by Hylesford School. Ten children with severe learning difficulties, aged eleven to fourteen, and their teacher, Jenny Wilson, were involved.

The Wolfson basement gallery contains Graeco-Roman sculpture of 200 BC–AD 200.

It consists of funerary statuary, grave reliefs, sarcophagi, mythological and historical figures. Jenny took some excellent photographs in the Wolfson Gallery which she used to prepare her group for their visit. She discussed the marble figures and some of the gods and goddesses which they portrayed.

The big foot

The sculptures in the Wolfson Basement are particularly large and seem to be asking to be touched. For conservation reasons, however, they may not be touched except by visually impaired visitors for whom there are special facilities. We wanted to see if the children could resist the temptation to touch, and whether it would adversely affect their enjoyment of the objects.

Jenny dealt with the conservation question in advance of the visits by stressing the importance of not touching, explaining that the sculptures could survive better for future generations of children like them. Chitra Aloysius met the children and was greeted by one of them, who had been on earlier trips to the National Gallery. He recalled this and said, 'I have seen the paintings of Monet and Van Gogh, and now I

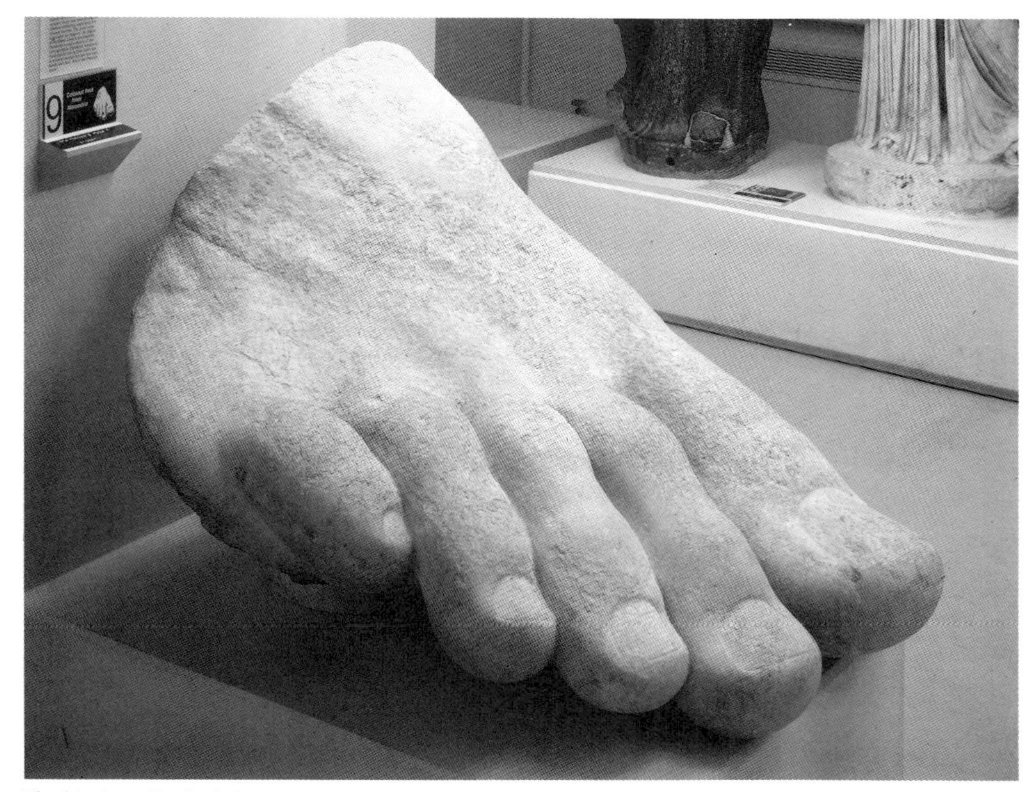

The big foot. To the left is a Braille label and small drawing of the object for visually impaired visitors.

want to see some statues and a big foot'. This remark showed that the child recalled vividly his earlier visit to the National Gallery and also that his preparatory work had been effective.

The 'big foot' was a great success. It is a very large marble foot, all that remains from an enormous statue from Alexandria in Egypt. The children had seen photographs of it in class, but were unprepared for its true size, and greeted it with great admiration and pleasure. Surprisingly it was not too difficult to dissuade them from touching it, even though it is, of all the sculptures in the gallery, perhaps the one that is most tempting. Jenny's emphasis in advance on not touching proved to be quite effective. The children did not attempt to touch, and indeed were so affected by the visual impact of the sculptures that they did not seem to need to touch.

Because so many of the sculptures are of deities with arms raised in dramatic gestures, a number of the children responded by mimicking them and attempting to strike similar poses. A dance project could use this gallery as a source of inspiration. It could be an excellent way of facilitating another kind of creative expression in a museum context, and not only for children with learning difficulties.

On leaving the gallery, after an hour and ten minutes, one of the children, Nicola, said goodbye to her favourite pieces by blowing them kisses.

Nicola and Jangia mimic a sculptural pose.

The lady lying down

A week later the group made their second visit. With them came Murtaza, who had not been able to come the first time. He was anxious to catch up with the others and like them had been well prepared in class. On the way to the galleries he asked Chitra to show him 'the lady who is lying down and the man with the necklace on his head'. (See illustrations below and on pp. 47 and 50.)

On the way to the Wolfson Basement Chitra tried to interest him in the massive Assyrian sculptures which they were passing, but he was too eager to get to the Roman sculptures, and said, 'They are nice but I must see the lady lying down'.

On their first visit the children had simply familiarised themselves with the gallery. This had been followed up at school with discussion sessions and sculpture workshops using plaster and sand as materials. On their second visit they were invited to select an object to draw. The foot and the Townley dogs (see page 56) proved the most popular. Murtaza went to his 'lady lying down' and spent some time viewing her from all angles before starting to draw. He seemed lost in a world of his own, gazing at the sculpture and struggling to record his impressions in his notebook.

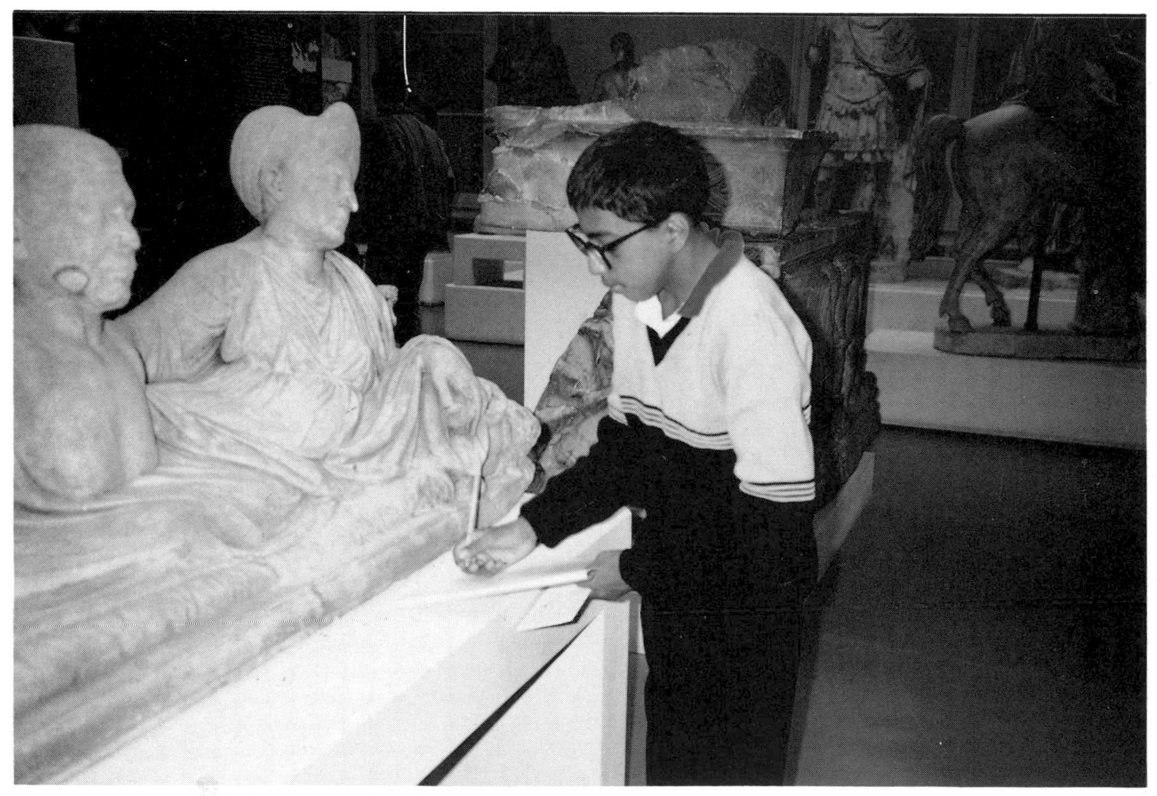

Murtaza and the 'lady lying down'.

Murtaza's drawing. He has incorporated the object number (bottom left) into his decorative scheme.

Roman sarcophagus cover; the wife holds a bust of her deceased husband.

(*Left*) Child's drawing of Thalia, 'the lady holding a stick, leaves and grapes in her hair'.
(*Right*) Life-size sculpture of Thalia, the Muse of Comedy.

Emma was impressed with a caryatid which she drew with great concentration and success (see p. 49). Jaswinder had great difficulty with drawing, but seemed to enjoy wandering around the sculptures, examining them closely. He showed his delight in the museum experience by kissing the gallery warder before leaving! Nurhan, who had seemed afraid of some of the larger figures on his first visit relaxed this time, commenting on them and attempting to draw.

Augustus cameo

At the end of the drawing session Murtaza remembered that he wanted to see the cameo of Augustus which he had seen on a postcard as part of the classroom preparation for the visit. As the group was leaving the Wolfson Gallery he approached

1 Classroom work based on the museum visit.

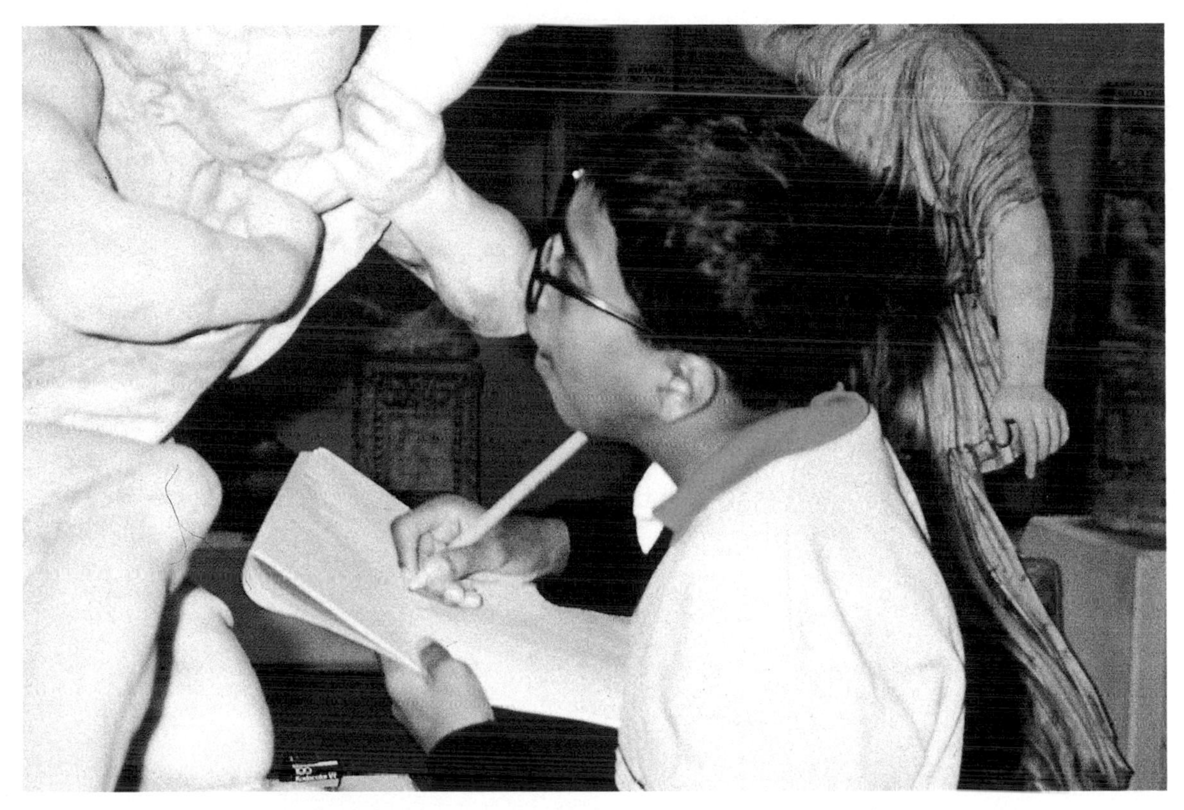

2 Children related closely and directly to certain objects.

3 This figure of a goat from the ancient Mesopotamian site of Ur evoked a strong response (see pp 52–3).

4 Gilded wooden coffin of an Egyptian priestess. This large and striking object was popular with the children from Beckton School.

5 The Roman mosaic bird which inspired the drawing reproduced on page 39.

6 Very much at home in the gallery.

The caryatid. The child has successfully captured the pose and mood of the figure in a few lines.

Murtaza admires the 'man with the necklace on his head'.

Jewelled cameo of the Emperor Augustus, in the upper Roman gallery.

another of the gallery warders and asked, 'Where can I find the man with the necklace on his head?' Supplied only with this information, the warder was able to direct him to the appropriate gallery!

This gallery was some considerable distance away and involved quite a long journey to the upper floor. Having found the object, Murtaza admired it, commented on the colours of the jewelled 'crown' and had his photograph taken in front of it.

THE ASSYRIANS

John F. Kennedy School from Stratford, East London, visited the Assyrian Galleries. These galleries contain carved stone slabs from the palace walls of ancient Nimrud, Khorsabad and Nineveh. They include battle scenes and lion hunts and give an amazingly detailed and often naturalistic picture of the Assyrian world of the ninth to the seventh centuries BC.

Seven children aged thirteen to fourteen with severe learning difficulties took part with their teacher, Angela Welman. Two of the children needed constant attention. They were John, who was very disturbed and needed to be held at all times, and Pali, who was most reluctant to participate.

Scene from an Assyrian relief, from Nimrud.

It had been suggested by the BMES co-ordinator that this group should engage in a study of Assyrian palace sculpture because of the dramatic narrative quality of the friezes and their successful use by mainstream children. Angela felt that the material would not appeal to the pupils because it was monocolour and therefore not attractive or easily visible to the children who had poor vision. The prohibition on touching the reliefs was also thought to be a problem.

After a brief introduction to the Assyrian palace sculpture, Chitra therefore decided that it would be better to visit the Wolfson basement which had already been tried and tested successfully with Hylesford School. Most of the group enjoyed the sculptures, especially the 'big foot', but John was very restless and they had to move on.

Chitra took them two floors up to Room 56, the Early Mesopotamian Room, to look at the goat with his forelegs resting on a tree, often called the Ram in the Thicket because it was thought to be inspired by the biblical story of Abraham and Isaac (see colour plate 3). The children, despite being completely unprepared for it, responded well to the goat, to the variety of colours used in it, to the shape of the tree and the fact that the goat on its hind legs seemed to be looking out at them. Chitra then took them to the Mozart exhibition so that they could listen to music through headphones.

Although the subject of this visit was changed at the last moment, and the children's response to museum objects was limited, they seemed to enjoy the experience which served as a good introduction for them. They would have undoubtedly derived more pleasure had they concentrated on one area with a specific task to do. John and Pali seemed to gain little from the visit and it might have been better if they had not taken part. This highlights the need for specific consultation before a visit is made and for careful consideration of the needs of each child. A visit to an unfamiliar place, removed from what may be the comforting and controlling limits of a familiar environment, can be stressful for some children, with or without learning difficulties. Teachers of mainstream children may sometimes have to decide not to include particular children in a group if they might make the visit unworkable.

THE VIKINGS

The British Museum has an important but limited range of Viking artefacts. The children looked at late Saxon and Viking jewellery and the characteristic tortoise brooches and some Viking tools and weapons. The students came from Arbour Vale School, a group of twelve young adults (aged sixteen–nineteen) all with severe learning difficulties. Their teacher/co-ordinator was Debs Aram.

They had visited the Jorvik Centre in York and were enthusiastic about Viking culture and clear about what they liked. One of the group announced on arrival, 'I want to see the Vikings and that is why we are here'.

The subject of the Vikings had been very much Debs' choice, rather against the advice of the BMES. The British Museum collection of Viking artefacts is not dramatically displayed, and is of more interest to the specialist. It was therefore felt that it would not appeal to these students. Mainstream primary schoolchildren aged seven–eleven use this material in working to the National Curriculum section called 'Invaders and Settlers' and sometimes encounter difficulty with it. In fact Debs had anticipated her students' response to this material and made detailed and clear preparation. In the gallery the students dispersed quickly, looking for particular examples of Viking objects like those which they had seen at the Jorvik Centre and which they had subsequently recreated at school.

Michael, for example, went looking for swords, Shifti surveyed the pottery and Mari was fascinated by the jewellery. Their response was brief and nonverbal, but real, reflecting a genuine recognition process. Debs was very satisfied with this response. Part of the success of the visit may well have been the earlier visit to the Jorvik Centre which provided the children with an intelligible and exciting context for the fragments of Viking culture they encountered in glass cases at the British Museum.

CHAPTER FOUR

Reflecting on the project

The children's reactions to the British Museum are described in some detail in the last chapter. These varied considerably from school to school and from child to child. Not every visit was an unqualified success. The following is an attempt to summarise achievements and problems.

ACHIEVEMENTS AND PROBLEMS

Aesthetic response

One of the benefits of an aesthetic approach to study is that it can facilitate a spontaneous response to sense experience. Instead of concentrating on factual description, the student becomes aware of the possibility of a wide range of emotional responses to different art forms.

As a result of working with the children in this project we have come to the conclusion that they have developed a degree of understanding of the nature of the ancient world and an awareness of what a museum is. They have also manifestly been able to enjoy objects for their own sake. We also believe that some children with severe learning difficulties may respond to objects more powerfully and imaginatively than mainstream pupils. 'Able' children who revel in the process of acquiring, sorting and expressing facts may indeed find the visual stimulation of museum objects a wonderful springboard for learning. However, they may be so concerned with acquiring factual information about objects and their cultural context, that they fail to look closely at the object and engage with it. The children who took part in the project, unfettered by any demand to slot the objects into a time frame or cultural preconceptions, responded with a much greater intensity to the objects themselves. It is, of course, difficult to measure precisely the degree of aesthetic response, especially in pupils who do not have highly developed verbal skills, but there was a quality of pure wonder which characterised the way they interacted with the objects.

Nicola responding to the Discus-thrower, in the Wolfson basement gallery.

This response was not the same for every child. In Chapter 3 we saw that some children did not react, or responded only in a limited way. It should also be emphasised that the amount of help which they received in preparation for their museum visit was much greater than the vast majority of children receive. Nevertheless, all the teacher/co-ordinators were surprised and impressed by the degree of enjoyment which the children got from their museum visits.

A sense of time

The children's sense of history and the dimension of time was clearly enhanced by their experiences, most of them developing a clearer understanding of the past and the differences between 'then' and 'now' as a result of their museum experience. They may not have comprehended the idea of varying interpretations about the past but they did sense the difference between real and imaginary (i.e. mythical) people. They were very aware that the objects they were looking at were made in the past, and they

(*Below*) Roman sculpture of two dogs (known as the Townley dogs) in the Wolfson basement gallery. (*Right*) The child has reproduced the sculptor's sensitive depiction of the two animals.

were able to comment on them and distinguish, for example, Greek from Egyptian material on grounds of style. Some also acquired a limited vocabulary range relating to the periods and themes being studied, e.g. mosaic, sculpture, gods.

To touch or not to touch

Another important point that emerged was that, with careful preparation, children with severe learning difficulties do not need to touch museum objects in order to appreciate them. This is particularly important for work in the British Museum because considerations of security and conservation prohibit the touching of most objects. Some of the children did want to touch, however, especially in the Roman sculpture galleries where some of the pieces are very accessible. Touch is an important element in appreciating museum objects and more touch facilities should be made available wherever possible. However, the vast majority of museum objects simply cannot be exposed to touch. If children with learning difficulties were to be confined to the few objects that can be touched they would be cut off from most of the main collections. Our experience is that they, like other children, can respond well to visual stimuli alone.

Social empowerment

The project contributed to the social empowerment of all the children. Terry Kilburn, head of the Castle School commented,

We would have not selected the British Museum for our children and may not have thought of ancient Greece as a suitable subject. I was pleasantly surprised by the response of the children and their involvement. Since taking part in the project, we have extended our study to ancient Rome. Most of the children showed emotional response to the artefacts. The study has given a lift to our children. The positive experience of the British Museum project has helped us to take on board the belief that our children can benefit from museum visits. We have since taken groups to all the museums.

Terry Kilburn also said that what was supposed initially to be a small scale project eventually involved the whole school, through the Greek banquet. He referred to a colleague who was inspired to write to Athens University in search of the ancient recipe for lentil stew which was cooked and served by the children at the feast (see Chapter 3).

The advantages of a second museum visit

The children felt more at ease with the museum on the second visit, and quickly settled down to work. They greeted the objects as old friends and were less shy of the gallery warders who sometimes remembered them and said hello. They were more verbal too, sometimes asking questions about certain objects, such as, 'What has happened to the head?'

Europe of the Rivers
After their initial expedition to the museum, the children from Beckton school continued to expand their social confidence via visits out of school. They visited France on two occasions. First they took part in the festival 'Europe of the Rivers' in Paris (see below), and then they went to see Monet's famous garden at Giverny (see Chapter 3).

The participation of the Beckton and Castle children in the British Museum project led to their being invited, as British representatives, to the European arts festival 'Europe of the Rivers'. This was organised by the education staff of the Ile de France Museum near Paris. Children from thirty-two countries were invited to Sceaux, a beautiful château in Nanterre, where they took part in a wide-ranging programme of arts activities including visiting museums and art galleries in Paris. The pupils from Beckton and Castle Schools were the only participants with learning difficulties. They flew to Paris from the City Airport in London by special arrangement with Brymon Airways. For all of them it was their first experience of foreign travel, which they adapted to very well, and enjoyed. Their artwork was exhibited in Paris.

THE BRITISH MUSEUM SEMINAR, NOVEMBER 1991

On Saturday 16 November, as the teaching and museum visiting phase of the project was drawing to a close, a seminar was held at the BMES. It had a dual purpose: to report on the progress of the project and to provide an opportunity for drawing parallels with similar projects in the USA. Renee Wells, whose pioneering work is described in Chapter 6, was invited to London and gave a presentation entitled 'An American Perspective' (see Chapter 6.)

Hazel Moffat HMI then chaired a panel discussion which focused on the cultural and educational rights of children with special needs; their right, for example, to participate in the National Curriculum and the entitlement of all children to visit national collections in museums and galleries. The panel was composed of Carolyn Keen, the Disability Adviser at the Museums and Galleries Commission, Renee Wells, and the project co-ordinators.

The value of this discussion was that it facilitated a valuable sharing of ideas between museum educators and classroom teachers about the educational needs of children in relation to museum collections. It was agreed that more training of teachers in this area was required and that more educational resources and informal advice networks should be set up.

CHAPTER FIVE

Other British projects

The pattern of work with learning difficulties at other museums and galleries is varied. Emphasis has been laid on the needs of schoolchildren, although there is now a growing recognition of the part museums can play in enriching the leisure time of adults with learning difficulties. The Government policy of care in the community means that there are many more people living outside protective institutions and likely to respond well to museums when imaginative provision is made for them.

The following examples have been chosen because they illustrate different ways of meeting the need and point the way forward to further development. The themes explored are as follows:

- Integration of learning disabled with mainstream children, (the Horniman Museum).
- Use of gallery space for exhibitions produced by community groups (Carousel and the Smith Art Gallery and Museum, Stirling).
- The importance of outreach programmes (the Dulwich Picture Gallery).
- Training of special needs teachers in the use of a particular museum collection (the Russell-Cotes Art Gallery and Museum, Bournemouth).
- Museum collections as inspiration for creative writing (Sunderland Museum and Art Gallery).

THE HORNIMAN MUSEUM, LONDON

The Horniman Museum in South London deals with the study of people and their environment. It has natural history and ethnographic collections as well as a newly-designed aquarium. There is a large collection of musical instruments from all over the world. The Horniman has a long tradition of educational programmes for both adults and children and Education staff have worked for several years with the staff and pupils of a nearby special school. Greenvale School caters for children with severe learning difficulties. Originally a school for children of all age ranges, it now has pupils between the ages of eleven and nineteen-plus.

Greenvale School places emphasis on integrated learning with pupils from local mainstream schools with whom Greenvale children often visit the museum. Like other special schools, Greenvale follows the National Curriculum which provides a useful framework for children to acquire a number of skills. These include choice, decision-making, responsibility of the students for themselves and others, as well as social awareness and confidence.

The Horniman Education Centre has always concentrated on handling museum objects as an aid to museum-based learning, for all school groups. For children with learning difficulties the handling experience is regarded as particularly important.

A musical approach

The museum's collection of musical instruments is used most effectively with the mixed groups of mainstream and learning disabled children. The latter can gain valuable tactile and auditory experiences, while the former may also concentrate on how the instruments are constructed, and the way in which the sounds are produced.

This work with mixed ability groups at the Horniman demonstrates how museum objects can enable children with learning difficulties to share an educational experience with other children. The response to a musical instrument does not necessarily require verbal skill. A learning disabled child may well be more sensitive to the actual sound of the instrument, and perhaps less self-conscious about actually playing it in a group.

Puppets and performance

The Horniman also has a good collection of hand, string and rod puppets. These can be used in a variety of ways and lend themselves well to teaching integrated groups of children. They encourage close observation and concentration skills for all ability levels; they are also helpful in language development as the children describe their construction, shape and colour. Problem solving and motor skills are used in understanding how to make the puppets move and then in manipulating them. The final puppet shows develop theatrical and musical skills and social confidence.

Paper fish

The new aquarium at the Horniman is similarly versatile. While, for example, one group may focus on looking at the fish as an inspiration for designs with which to decorate papier-mâché pots, others may use the exhibit as a valuable source of scientific and ecological information.

CAROUSEL

Carousel is an organisation based in the south-east of England which promotes the active participation of people with learning difficulties in the arts through workshops, residencies, performances and exhibitions. It is funded from a variety of sources including the Arts Council of England, the South-East Arts Association and the local borough council and health authority.

Carousel operates in day-centres, hospitals and schools and explores music, visual art, drama, dance and movement. In 1992 Carousel organised a project at St. Helen's Museum in Lancashire as part of a Special Needs Arts Festival. In just eight days, clients, carers, Carousel workers and museum staff produced an exhibition on the theme of home life.

Initial workshops encouraged the participants to explore personal feelings about their own homes through visual art, music and drama. These fed in to the production of the exhibition itself which took the form of a series of room sets – a kitchen, sitting-room, bathroom and garden – constructed mainly of scrap materials. The finished product was a highly imaginative piece of visual art and a fine example of how gallery space can be made available successfully to disadvantaged groups.

A spokesperson for Carousel remarked,

Raising the profile of creative-arts work by people with learning difficulties is one of Carousel's main aims, but unfortunately there are few public platforms for this kind of work to be shown. Housing such an exhibition in a mainstream venue like St. Helen's Museum added much to the value of the finished work, in which the participants took so much pride.[1]

THE SMITH ART GALLERY AND MUSEUM, STIRLING

In March 1990 the main temporary exhibition gallery of this museum was given over to a multi-arts project specifically organised for disabled people. The space (30m × 12m) was transformed into a rain forest environment, complete with river, ceremonial hut, forest trees and animals. This was another good example of gallery space being used creatively by groups of people with disabilities.

THE DULWICH PICTURE GALLERY

The Dulwich Picture Gallery, England's oldest public picture gallery, was opened in 1817. It is an elegant single-storey building surrounded by lawns opposite Dulwich Park in south London.

It was established with a dual purpose, to display its important collection of seventeenth and eighteenth century paintings and to play a part in the local community. It continues this tradition today, in spite of the limitations on its resources. It has no teaching room or special equipment and only a small educational budget of £1,000 a year, plus a few thousands more from private sponsorship, notably Marks and Spencer.

Nevertheless, the Gallery has developed a high quality educational service by the imaginative use of its building and collections, including very good provision for special needs groups. These include children with moderate and severe learning difficulties, and with emotional and behavioural problems. The programmes, which are organised by a specialist teacher who is also an art historian, involve outreach sessions at schools and day centres. The normal pattern is an introductory visit to the school, followed by the gallery visit and, if requested, a follow-up visit by the teacher to the school.

Every year there is an art competition based on the pictures in the Gallery, and there are prizes in every category of special need and age-group.

THE RUSSELL-COTES ART GALLERY AND MUSEUM, BOURNEMOUTH

This museum has impressive collections of Victorian art and world cultural material. These are complemented by contemporary art and craft commissions. It won a National Heritage award for the best Fine Art museum in the UK in 1991. A project known as 'Arts for All' was established at the Russell-Cotes Art Gallery and Museum in the same year. Its purpose was to encourage pupils with learning difficulties to use the museum as a creative resource. Most of the pupils had moderate learning difficulties, although one group had severe learning difficulties.

Louise Evans, Arts Development Officer, was inspired to start the project by a course she attended at the Centre for Disability and the Arts in Leicester. The Russell-Cotes Art Gallery and Museum hosted the Centre's exhibition 'Finding Form: Sculpture to Touch' and held sculpture workshops for children with special needs in conjunction with it.

The experience highlighted the potential of the museum to draw out latent abilities in children with learning difficulties. It also revealed the need to provide training in the use of museums for teachers of children with special educational needs.

A programme was set up and jointly funded by Bournemouth Borough Council and Dorset Education Authority. It was devised by a planning team composed of the Arts Development Officer, two members of the Special Educational Needs Advisory team, and Dance and Music specialists from the Creative and Expressive Arts team. This combination of expertise proved to be invaluable.

The Special Educational Needs team's ability to draw on its network of contacts in schools was also vital, as the initial response to the publicity for the course was slow. Ultimately, eight teachers and seventy five pupils from five special schools across

Dorset participated. Four sessions took place over a five month period from November 1992 to March 1993. The initial one introduced teachers to different ways of working with artefacts and allowed them to negotiate their individual objectives. The second session involved a full day for teachers at the museum, with workshops led by the Creative and Expressive Arts Team and by the Arts Development Officer. In the third session the pupils worked with the teachers in the museum to develop dance, music and drama pieces. The final workshop provided a forum for both teachers and facilitators to evaluate the project and consider the way forward.

Interaction of objects and art form

The stimulus for work was provided by a variety of artefacts. A mobile contemporary sculpture was used as a focus by the pupils and teachers, who translated its sweeping abstract forms into movements and simple dance sequences. Masks from Japan and Nigeria were used to inspire mood, rhythm and symmetry in music. Perceptions of non-western cultures were also explored and the use of stereotyped imagery discouraged.

A Victorian painting of a beach at sunset proved to be a rich source of inspiration. The pupils created imaginary identities for the painted figures, including a band of smugglers and a courting couple. They wrote appropriate dialogues for the characters and acted out the different scenes. One child played the artist working on the painting and brought the groups of characters to life in sequence. The scenes were orchestrated into a tableau by their teacher and given a chanting refrain with the help of the Music Advisory teacher. The pupils were so absorbed in the project that they continued working on it outside school hours.

One of the teachers commented:

I had hoped that the pupils would understand how an artefact can provide the stimulus for living artistic experience. They certainly achieved this, and I was pleased to see how quickly they bridged the gap between concrete and abstract ideas.

SUNDERLAND MUSEUM AND ART GALLERY

In Spring 1993 Sunderland Museum and Art Gallery hosted 'A Fresh Look', an exhibition selected from the permanent collection of twentieth century British Art at Middlesborough Art Gallery. As part of the education programme, Sunderland Museum invited poet Sue Kane to run a series of workshops using the pictures as a stimulus for the creation of poems. These were advertised to special schools and proved very successful.

Many of the students in the workshops could neither read nor write, but all had ideas and insights into the pictures which were incorporated into group poems. At the end of the exhibition all the groups came back to the museum for a final poetry reading.

The following are a selection of some of the poems.

Mabel Cherriman of Ditchling by Eric Gill.

Eric Gill: *Mabel Cherriman of Ditchling.*

In her eyes and on her mouth,
She shows her broken heart.

Poem by Margaret Sutton School, South Shields.

L.S. Lowry: *People on a Pavement*

Waiting for a Bus

Bad man he should not be,
He is.
He should not be, should not be,
Smoking a pipe.
Bad man in a funny hat,
Waiting, waiting.
Waiting an awful long time,
Waiting for a bus.

Poem by High Fell School, Gateshead.

Josef Herman: *Morning*

Jesus Painting

A Jesus painting, with a sunrise waiting.
Women in robes,
A tired donkey plodding on,
A winding road.

Poem by Sunningdale School, Sunderland.

Morning by Josef Herman.

REFERENCES

1. Moore, Kevin, 'Open House, Open Mind', *Museums Journal*, March 1993.

CHAPTER SIX

The American experience

Forty three million Americans, amounting to 17 per cent of adults and children, have some kind of disability. Although they have become a part of mainstream society over the past decade, they are far from being truly integrated. A series of changes in legislation has brought about improvements in services for disabled visitors to museums in the USA, but as in Britain, provision tends to be patchy and variable.

LEGISLATION

A number of federal laws govern accessibility. In 1968 the Architectural Barriers Act became law. This concerns architectural accessibility in buildings constructed with the assistance of federal funds.

In 1973 the Rehabilitation Act was passed. It provided technical assistance and enforcement of federal accessibility statutes. Section 504 of the Act states:

No otherwise qualified handicapped individual in the US ... shall, solely by reasons of his handicap, be excluded from the participation in, be denied the benefits of, or be subjected to discrimination under any program or activity receiving federal financial assistance.

The section 504 regulations are the result of a vigorous civil rights movement organised by a coalition of disabled people. Employment discrimination against people with disabilities is legislated against by human rights laws.

All this legislation has ensured a baseline of provision for disabled people in all publicly funded institutions, including museums. It has had a profound effect on professional practice in America and on the lives of disabled people. More recent legislation has reinforced the impetus towards equality and accessibility.

The Americans with Disabilities Act of July 1992 is, in effect, a civil rights charter for disabled people and the first of its kind in the world. It provides for individual rights in employment, education, public services, transport and housing. It forbids any government body or employer with over fifteen workers to discriminate against a qualified disabled person simply on the grounds of disability.

Where there are already stringent accessibility laws, the main impact of this latest Act is likely to be the heightened awareness that it will generate. Arts organisations will come under far closer scrutiny from advocacy organisations, as well as from disabled individuals. All the advisory documentation provided with the Act strongly advises arts organisations to ensure that they are fully accessible, in terms of architecture, employment and programmes on offer.

Although museums have had to comply with Section 504 regulations in order to receive federal funding, the regulations do not stipulate specific methods for accomplishing this and indeed allow as much flexibility in compliance with the legislation as possible.

Mandatory access to a museum's programmes and services presents a challenge to arts professionals. In many cases provision for disabled visitors requires more imagination than expense, more ingenuity than equipment. Under this legislative umbrella many short term projects focusing on the needs of people with learning difficulties have come into being.

The question of museum funding has an important bearing on development. The funding of museums in the USA is much more complex than it is in Britain. Museums which roughly correspond to the national museums of the UK, e.g. the Metropolitan Museum in New York, receive some federal funding. However, many museum functions, especially educational provision for disabled visitors, are funded by a variety of different agencies. These include commercial benefactors, private sponsors and disability organisations which occasionally finance programmes and temporary exhibitions.

Educational facilities for people with learning disabilities, especially for children and young adults, are generally more widespread in American museums than in the UK. This may be the result of the more flexible staffing arrangements including the use of docents (trained volunteers) which obtain in America. It is generally easier to second qualified and experienced special needs classroom teachers to train and work alongside museum staff on museum based projects.

THE BRITISH MUSEUM PROJECT: AMERICAN LINKS

The British Museum project had useful links with American curators and teachers working with children with learning difficulties in museums. A pioneer in this field in New York and Massachusetts is Renee Wells who came to England to speak at the British Museum Project Seminar in November 1991. Renee Wells is the co-founder of the Access Network for Museums USA (see below) and Director of Education and Outreach at the Children's Art Exchange in Middlebury, Vermont. The Children's Art Exchange is a multi-cultural organisation serving the USA and the former Soviet Union. Its purpose is to enable children in these countries to learn about each other through participation in the arts.

The Access Network for Museums

The Access Network was set up in the USA in February 1988 and like MAGDA, the Museums and Galleries Disability Association in the UK, acts as a forum for museum professionals interested in access programmes for people with disabilities. A major plank of the work of the Access Network is in the area of learning disability. Advocacy groups of people with learning disabilities help museum staff in the devising of facilities and services.

At the BM seminar Renee Wells provided an overview of some museum work in the USA with children with learning difficulties and made a number of suggestions for future development based on her experience:

This work can be applied in ways which help all museum visitors. Museums are appropriate places where social responses of various kinds may occur naturally. They are 'empowering' places in the sense that visitors can express themselves in a very individual way. Unlike the classroom perhaps, there is no 'right' or 'correct' response. Some people with learning difficulties feel liberated by a museum environment.

In America there are regular programmes which consciously build on the experience of earlier work and expand upon it. In spite of their high quality, these are often low-cost projects, partly because they are undertaken by docents, highly trained volunteers who are an important feature of museum interpretation in the USA.

Guidelines for teachers are recognised to be of great importance, as they are in Britain. They should provide, together with contextual information about the objects to be seen, practical advice to help teachers to prepare their students for the visit. Since, for many children with learning difficulties, their visit may well be the first to a museum, it is necessary to make clear to them that no unexpected demands will be made on them, and that they will not be placed in a situation which makes them feel exposed or vulnerable. Maps, directional information and approximate costs of the visit are all useful information which the teacher should be given in advance.

Renee also recommended that museums should devise special educational integrated programmes which draw on the strengths of their own collections and the ideas and philosophies behind their displays. In the USA, as elsewhere, the terminology of disability is in a constant state of evolution. The American equivalent of the term 'learning disabilities', currently used in Britain, is 'specific learning disabilities' and 'developmental delay'. Several American museums have programmes for children with learning differences, who usually take part in them with friends, staff and other family members. The following are just a few examples.

THE METROPOLITAN MUSEUM, NEW YORK

The Metropolitan Museum of Art in New York's Fifth Avenue is the largest art museum in the western hemisphere. In addition to its great collections of European paintings, it has outstanding holdings of Medieval art and architecture as well as prints, photographs, drawings, costumes, musical instruments, sculpture and decorative arts from antiquity to the twentieth century.

At the Metropolitan, students with disabilities are invited to participate in all the Museum's education programmes. In addition, there is a group of docents who specialise in working with students with learning disabilities, emotional, behavioural and developmental disabilities.

Connie Cummings, an Education Officer at the Metropolitan Museum, writes, 'Many of the students have poor reading skills, maths may seem like a foreign language and spelling overwhelms them, but when it comes to looking, enjoying and learning from works of art, they are as capable as any other visitors to the Museum'.

The programme starts with a brief slide introduction in a Museum classroom, followed by a gallery tour. The groups are kept deliberately small, with no more than nine students per docent.

The docent involves the students by asking them open questions which do not depend on prior knowledge to be able to answer. The docents also provide comparative information which will help the students to relate to what they are being shown. For example, when looking at a seventeenth century period room, they may ask, 'How is this room different from your room at home?'

This method of interpretation actively engages the students, increases their visual skills and allows for the necessary flexibility in working with students at various academic levels. It is a teaching technique which creates a positive, participatory museum tour which is successful with all students, not only those with learning disabilities.

The Museum has, for some years, run a series of weekend workshops, entitled 'Discoveries', for developmentally disabled people and their families. Each concentrates on a special theme, e.g. 'line, shape and colour', or 'tombs, temples and treasures', and includes a guided gallery tour and a related art activity e.g. adornment with Egyptian-inspired jewellery designed in the practical workshop part of the programme.

The Metropolitan Museum of Art has also produced a very useful booklet, *Museums: A Resource for the Learning Disabled*. It is based on extensive work with groups of adults and children with learning difficulties and explains why museums are appropriate resources for them:

. . . If a child is dyslexic, he may have difficulty in comprehending and completing a classroom reading assignment. Or if a child has problems understanding the spoken word, he might not benefit fully from a teacher's oral presentation. During a museum visit however, such children can obtain information directly by looking at an exhibit as they listen to the guide's descriptive explanation. Combining visual and aural input can be an effective means of teaching because it compensates for deficiencies that may result from the processing of information.

Experts in the field emphasise that museums provide an opportunity for teachers to work with a child's special strengths and interests. Many learning disabled students, for instance, are strong in visual and spatial areas. They need to acquire knowledge from actual three-dimensional objects before they can understand abstract concepts, and the objects on view in a museum can allow for this 'concrete' learning process to take place. Although many learning disabled children have a poor sense of time, a museum can provide examples of time sequences, such as objects throughout history or from a specific time period.[1]

At the Metropolitan some docents specialised in working with students with learning difficulties. Gradually however it became apparent that many of the lessons learnt from working with such children and adults had a wider application, i.e. they could provide valuable insights into mainstream educational work. Now all docents participate in the teaching of special needs groups and indeed such participation is seen as an essential source of inspiration for mainstream teaching and interpretation. Slide talks are often used as introductions to a museum visit for children with special educational needs.

There have been experiments, too, with the method of using just one slide of one museum object and dealing with different aspects of it. An example has an Egyptian object as its subject. It is dealt with in four parts: The Afterlife, Written Images, The Gods and The Kings. Each single slide is accompanied by ten lines of text describing it. The text encourages the viewer to look closely at the object for some time, and from different angles. It also directs the viewer to other related objects in the galleries.

A variant of this method is a standard element in docent training. Objects are examined from different angles; from the point of view of their visual appearance, historical or artistic context, technical production etc. The information is then blended together and applied by the docent in ways which meet the differing needs of various groups.

The method, using one powerful image as a catalyst for a more in-depth study of a culture, seems to be especially effective in holding the attention of children with learning difficulties. We have attempted to apply this principle in the BMES Learning Difficulties Resource Pack.

THE MUSEUM OF FINE ARTS, BOSTON

The museum has comprehensive collections ranging from Europe and the Americas to Asia, from ancient civilisations to the present day. It has silver, furniture and portraits and French paintings. Eleanor Rubin of the Education Department is the co-ordinator of Special Services and provides a range of services for adults and children with disabilities.

Thematic gallery tours for very small groups of adults or children with special needs have proved successful. For example, a wide spectrum of objects, such as screens, scrolls, textiles and sculpture can be examined in a tour entitled 'A Field Trip to Asia'.

Other programmes have helped participants to develop skills of perceiving, exploring, reacting and relating to museum objects through sketching, story-telling and movement. An interesting link with the British Museum project is the emphasis laid on the value of making two museum visits. On the second visit the children are more familiar with the environment and this seems to be of great help to some groups, enabling them to feel much more at ease.

The museum also provides groups of children with canvas gallery-bags filled with objects that have some connection with a particular picture on display in the gallery. These might include cardboard 'samplers' with brush strokes in thick paint, paint-brushes, rocks which contain pigment elements, palates and colour samples and pieces of fabric. Gallery bags and other similar projects are often devised and produced by people from a range of interest groups, museum staff, parents, teachers and people with disabilities.

THE MUSEUM OF SCIENCE, BOSTON

In a few American museums the needs of disabled visitors have been fully integrated at an early stage in the planning of mainstream facilities. For example, at the Museum of Science in Boston the needs of people with learning disabilities have been taken into account in designing a gallery composed of traditional window dioramas (a display technique popular in the USA). The subject of the gallery is New England animal habitats. It is augmented with multisensory, interactive components.

Services for disabled visitors at the Science Museum owe much to the work of Betty Davidson, a biochemist and schoolteacher. In 1987 she co-ordinated an access assessment at the museum and since then, with the help of a grant from the National Science Foundation, has helped to plan science exhibitions for a broad spectrum of visitors, including those with disabilities.

A detailed evaluation of the preparation and use of the New England Habitats gallery in the Boston Museum has been published.[2] Much of the analysis concentrates on the needs of the sensorily impaired, which were carefully kept in mind in the consultation and preparation of the exhibition. However there are some particular features which can be considered here in relation to the needs of children with learning difficulties who are regular users of the gallery.

From the beginning the gallery was designed by a team of people who included museum staff, special needs consultants and specialists in programme research and evaluation. For the visitors with disabilities the key issues were primarily independence and information, whereas for the museum personnel they were considerations of durability, cost, physical and intellectual access and aesthetics, i.e. whether a particular approach is worth the time, trouble and expense. The final design features, in response to these disparate needs, involve careful attention to labels, and the use of activity stations.

Labels

Labels needed to be direct, short and linguistically clear, and to include explanations of technical terms. Large print, good colour contrast and lighting proved to be as important for visitors with learning difficulties as for those with visual impairments. Printed labels were two-tiered, with the most important information in very large print and supplementary information in somewhat smaller, but still large, print in a plain style.

Simple, easy-to-see graphics were included in the labels. Here is an example.

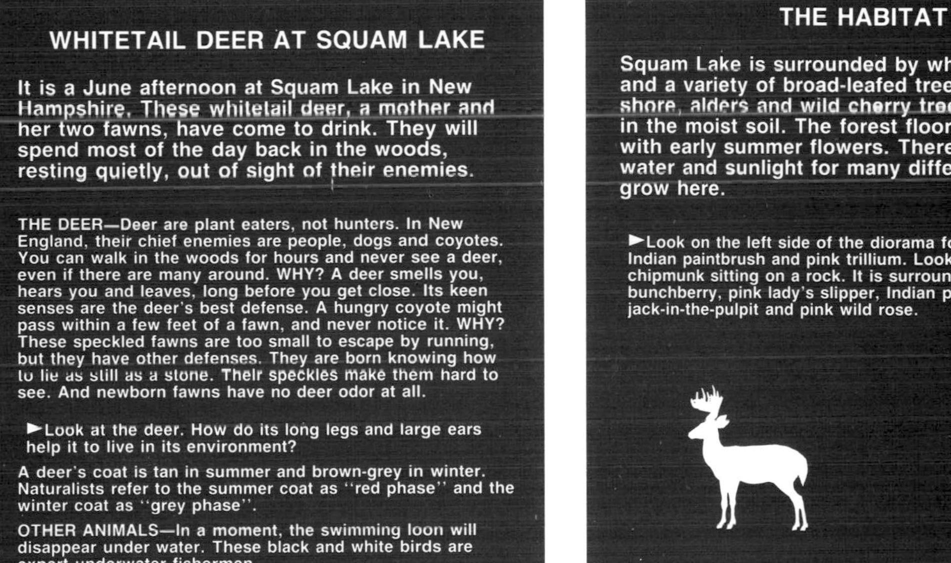

These findings and recommendations bear a remarkable similarity to those made by the British students with dyslexia about their visits to museums in Bristol in 1991. (See Chapter 7.)

Activity stations

The gallery also had three so-called 'activity stations' which tied the separate dioramas together, illustrating the common theme of animal adaptations. One had touchable fur samples illustrating the insulating and water-proofing qualities of some of the furry animals in the dioramas. The second was called the 'Animal Tools' activity station. Adaptive mouth and foot parts were paired with human tools which performed a similar function. The third, 'Build a Beast', consisted of shapes of different parts of an animal's body. The idea was to assemble an animal adapted to a particular lifestyle.

A group of nine to twelve year-old learning disabled boys explored the exhibition. Only two of them expressed a preference for the touch and smell design features. The other two said that they preferred just to look. This ties in with the experience of children with moderate and severe learning difficulties at the British Museum where tactile facilities were not available (see Chapter 3).

They found the activity stations rather confusing, but were able to talk about a key theme of the exhibition, the specific adaptive modifications of individual animals. For example they understood that beavers have teeth and tails as adaptive features, that bears have fur for warmth as well as claws for climbing trees, and that deer have long legs which enable them to run away from predators.

THE SMITHSONIAN INSTITUTION, WASHINGTON

The Smithsonian, with its fourteen museums and national zoo, is the world's largest museum complex. It holds some 134 million artefacts and specimens in its trust 'for the increase and diffusion of knowledge amongst men'. A leading research centre in the basic sciences, history and the arts, it was established in 1846 with funds bequeathed to the United States by James Smithson, an English scientist.

Services for disabled visitors at the Smithsonian are highly developed, partly because Washington, as the capital city, is also the headquarters of many of the federal organisations and national charities working with and on behalf of disabled people. This means that there are excellent communications between the museums and these advocate groups and large numbers of disabled people who live in the city are enthusiastic consumers of museum services.

One of the main contributions of the Education Service is the publication of a videotape and handbook *Part of Your General Public is Disabled* by Janice Majewski, which was published in 1987. The two resources are a comprehensive account of different kinds of disability and the associated physical and attitudinal barriers that prevent disabled people from enjoying the educational experiences that museums have to offer. The techniques required to make the necessary changes are described in detail in the book and discussed on the videotape with people with disabilities.[3]

THE ACCESSIBLE MUSEUM

The American Association of Museums has recently published a book entitled *The Accessible Museum: Model Programs of Accessibility for Disabled and Older People.* National Endowment for the Arts special co-ordinator, Paula Terry, describing the publication wrote,

It is about opening up existing programs and activities to older and disabled individuals in ways which promote human dignity. It is not just a question of complying with federal laws. These populations are vast potential markets for museums. They are collectively an economic force, an educated force, and potentially a cultural force.

The book profiles nineteen American museums with exemplary and varied access arrangements. They are grouped under four separate headings: unique outreach programmes, innovative solutions, broad-based programmes and training programmes.

The Children's Museum in Boston is a good example of those which have highly developed outreach programmes. It was a pioneer in devising exhibitions which expand the visitor's understanding of disability. In 1979 it held an exhibition called 'What if you couldn't?' which gave children and their families a deeper awareness of disability in childhood. Since then the museum has developed many services for children with disabilities and has a team of interpreters trained in integrating children with disabilities into the mainstream of museum education. Dyslexia is a particular area of focus.

The following list of museums involved in this kind of work shows the extent of current activity in a range of American museums:

The John Marlor Arts Centre, Milledgeville, Georgia
The Natural History Museum of Los Angeles County, California
The Spertus Museum of Judaica, Chicago, Illinois
The Aquarium of the Americas, New Orleans, Louisiana
The Bloedel Reserve, Bainbridge Island, Washington
Drayton Hall, Charleston, South Carolina
The Jim Buck Ross Mississippi Agriculture and Forestry National Agricultural Aviation Museum, Jackson, Mississippi
The Oakland Museum, Oakland, California

Winterthur Museum, Winterthur, Delaware
The Metropolitan Museum of Art, New York
The Museum of Fine Arts, Boston, Massachusetts
Old Sturbridge Village, Sturbridge, Massachusetts
The Fine Arts Museum, San Francisco, California
Kimbell Art Museum, Fort Worth, Texas
Lawrence Hall of Science, Berkeley, California
Museum of Science, Boston, Massachusetts
University Museum, South Illinois University, Carbondale, Illinois.

REFERENCES

1. *Museums: A Resource for the Learning Disabled*, Division of Education Service, The Metropolitan Museum of Art, New York, 1984.
2. *New Dimensions for Traditional Dioramas*, Betty Davidson, 1991
3. Majewski, J., *Part of Your General Public is Disabled* Smithsonian Institution, 1990
4. *The Accessible Museum: Model Programs of Accessibility for Disabled and Older People* American Association of Museums, 1992

FURTHER READING

Wells, Renee, 'Museums are for Everyone', *Their World: Journal of the Foundation for Children with Learning Disabilities*, 1991.
Wurtzel, Clare, 'Planning Museum Trips for Children with Learning Disabilities', *Their World: Journal of the Foundation for Children with Learning Disabilities*, 1988.

CHAPTER SEVEN

Suggestions and conclusions

The following are some general recommendations for development of facilities and services based on the work undertaken at the museum and comments made by others during the course of the project.

FACTORS FOR A SUCCESSFUL VISIT

The School

- Focused preparation with strongly visual resources and, ideally, a context into which the disparate museum displays can be placed (e.g. the mosaics in the local swimming pool at Stratford; a visit to the Jorvik Centre by the group studying the Vikings).
- Children have greater confidence when they can refer back to earlier experiences (e.g. Monet's lilies) and recognise specific objects to which they have been introduced in advance.
- The appeal of the visit may be the 'otherness' of museum collections, but there need to be familiar points of contact (e.g. food).
- A clear sense of purpose and structure is necessary but this should not preclude the chance to respond fully to children's reactions to material that was not included in the core visit.
- Consolidation of conclusions and connections during the visit is desirable to avoid confusion (especially in a big collection like the BM's) and to prompt further enquiry.
- Cross-curricular work is a great strength of many museum visits, even more so than in the mainstream curriculum (e.g. Egypt for art, history, English, technology); but the impact of the visit should not be diluted by trying to do too much.
- Enough well-prepared helpers are essential, especially if severely disabled children are included; trained volunteers may be needed as well.

- Whole-school support for the project yields considerable dividends (e.g. the Greek project culminating in a feast for the whole school).
- Freshness of perception on the visit can be recreated in the classroom with the use of cameras and tape recorders during the visit.

The museum

- Museum Education Departments need to develop stronger links with teachers of children with learning difficulties, making this area a specific responsibility for a particular member of the museum staff. Too often links are based on personal contacts only.
- In providing good preparatory material, Education Departments should consider not only the needs of teachers, but also good visual stimuli for discussion with children (e.g. postcard packs, posters etc.) and the potential of information technology where there are special opportunities for learning difficulties groups.
- Implications for museum design are discussed in Chapters 2 and 6 and below. Benefits to children and adults with learning difficulties will inevitably benefit everybody.
- Greater use of creative writing, dance and drama as a way of interpreting and experiencing museum collections.

RESULTS OF A SUCCESSFUL MUSEUM VISIT

- Greater motivation, not only in particular curriculum areas but for the school as a whole.
- Greater self-confidence for pupils in their ability to recognise, respond, make choices and decisions.
- Development of the specific learning skills of hand to eye co-ordination, concentration, observation through drawing.
- Powerful creative, aesthetic and emotional responses (rather than logical or analytical ones) which result in more concentrated work and language work, especially from students for whom English is a secon [illegible]guage.
- Enhanced social skills and confidence (e.g. the Rivers Project).
- Multicultural educational possibilities, especially for children from ethnic groups who are unaccustomed to visiting museums.
- Raised expectations of teachers.
- Encouragement of more museum visits on a regular basis.

PHYSICAL ACCESS

None of the children who participated in the British Museum project had ambulatory difficulties or were wheelchair users. If they had been, they would not have encountered too much difficulty because all the galleries that they used are wheelchair accessible. Most of the British Museum's public galleries are accessible, mainly because the museum was purpose built in the nineteenth century and designed with wide spaces to facilitate the moving of large pieces of ancient sculpture. More recently-established museums, occupying what were large private houses or industrial spaces, often have more testing access problems.

As the integration of children with special needs into mainstream education gathers momentum, access at museums will increasingly have to be taken into account when planning visits. Museums can help by providing access information in the form of a leaflet, describing the physical nature of the building in as much detail as possible; for example, the number of steps at the entrance and internally, and how many wheelchairs can be accommodated together in the lift.

These are important questions for every special needs teacher, because a carefully planned visit can be easily marred by time lost negotiating obstacles. Lunch rooms are also important. This was a problem at the British Museum, because the lunch room for schoolchildren is a good fifteen minutes' walk from the galleries, and therefore too far away to be of any practical use for many children with special needs.

A manual for teachers with practical information about visiting the museum should be available. It should include travel and parking arrangements, advice on the size of the group, number of escorts needed, lunch room facilities, advance and follow-up exercises.

EDUCATIONAL RESOURCES: WHAT CAN MUSEUMS PROVIDE?

Teachers of children with learning difficulties are expert at adapting all manner of resources for use with their pupils. There are few museum resources tailored to the needs of such children, but existing materials can be used. Those of the BMES were very helpful to the teacher/co-ordinators in preparing for the project, partly because they are specifically designed for teachers to adapt for their own purposes.

Museums need advice and criticism from special needs teachers to help them to improve provision generally. There is an urgent need to build up a body of experience and documentation about the reaction of children with learning disabilities to all types of museum collections, not only archaeological and art-historical, but also collections of natural history, social history and science and technology material.

The BMES has produced a Resource Pack to help teachers of children with learning difficulties to use the British Museum. It consists of worksheets and line drawings, suggestions for artwork and language development and is based on the experience of the Big Foot project co-ordinators. It concentrates on the galleries described in this

Ankhs & Waterlilies

Teachers' pack for use with children with learning difficulties

The work of the Big Foot project has generated a resource pack for special needs teachers, of which this is the front cover.

book, but also makes suggestions about other BM material which has proved successful with children with a wide range of creative abilities.

QUESTIONS OF DESIGN

Design factors are of great importance. The need for a simple and clear arrangement of objects and explanatory information was emphasised by some students with dyslexia who spoke at the British Museum Seminar in 1991. They drew attention to various areas of difficulty which they encounter at museums, including reading speeds and problems with decoding new and unfamiliar words. They are often faced by too much wall panel text.

Some dyslexic people have problems with visual memory and some with auditory memory; their concentration span may therefore be short. They may also be distracted by noise and fussy exhibits. Dyslexia sometimes causes difficulty with directionality, usually confusion about left and right, but sometimes also up and down and front and back. If steps are taken to alleviate these problems, especially in terms of improved design, exhibitions would be clearer and more enjoyable for everyone.

Greater use of headings and sub-headings to break up lengthy explanations can significantly enhance the reader's ability to scan text. 'Designer' panels of text, such as grey on blue, should be avoided. They present difficulties not only for people with dyslexia, but also those with visual impairments. Colour should be more frequently used to section and highlight text.

Printed plans to use in the museum are essential. Many visitors have difficulty remembering the directional information supplied in one central map.

A wide variety of interpretative material should be used: models, paintings, artefacts, photographs, videos (especially short videos). In this way visitors who may have difficulty retaining information visually can compensate by absorbing it aurally instead, and vice versa.

More hands-on experience would be helpful as would more widespread use of multi-sensory experience, tape-guides and videos.

As far as possible there should be greater and more imaginative use of all presentation methods which do not rely heavily on the written word.

APPENDIX 1

Schools which participated in the British Museum Project

Gurney School, Forest Gate, London Borough of Newham
Teacher/co-ordinator: Cheryl Chant

Hylesford School, Ilford, Essex
Teacher/co-ordinator: Jenny Wilson

Castle School, London Borough of Barking and Dagenham
Teacher/co-ordinator: Marion Price

John F. Kennedy School, Stratford, East London
Teacher/co-ordinator: Angela Welman

Arbour Vale School, Slough, Berkshire
Teacher/co-ordinator: Debs Aram

Beckton School, London Borough of Newham
Teacher/co-ordinator: Tim Miller

APPENDIX 2

Headteachers

The role of the headteachers and the co-ordinating teachers.
The headteachers of the six schools recognised the value of the project for their pupils and made it possible by releasing staff, obtaining parents' permission for the visit, and arranging transport and funds. We are particularly grateful to Maggie Angele, headteacher of Beckton school, for releasing Chitra Aloysius to the British Museum in order to co-ordinate the Project.

Headteachers
Maggie Angele, Beckton School
Doreen Ellmore, John F. Kennedy School
Helen McClennon, Gurney School
Terry Kilburn, Castle School
Judy Thrupp, Arbour Vale School
Jill Morgan, Hylesford School

APPENDIX 3

Consultants and advisers

Jane Holmes, Newham Arts Education Centre
Jenny Waterhouse, Newham Arts Education Centre
Jean MacIntyre, Primary Education Co-ordinator, Design Council
Jane Riches, Principal Lecturer in Art, Design and Architecture, University of East London
Dr Jenny Corbett, Senior Lecturer in Special Needs, University of East London
Phyllis Cottrell, Chair of the Board of Governors, Hylesford School.
Meg Henderson, TVEI Team, London Borough of Newham
Harvey Deslow, Eastlea Community School

APPENDIX 4

British Museum Press publications and British Museum Education Resources used for the Project

THE EGYPTIANS

BMP
Egyptians Activity Book
Hart, *Egyptian Myths*
Hart, *Eyewitness Ancient Egypt* (Dorling Kindersley/BMP)
Stead, *Egyptian Life*
Andrews, *Egyptian Mummies*
James, *Egyptian Painting*
James and Davies, *Egyptian Sculpture*
Taylor, *Egypt and Nubia*
Davies, *Egyptian Hieroglyphs*
Wilson, *Ancient Egyptian Designs*
Quirke and Spencer, *The British Museum Book of Ancient Egypt*

BMES Resources
Egypt pack and video
Hunt the Hieroglyphs Trail
Howard Carter exhibition pack

THE GREEKS

BMP
Greeks Activity Book
Burn, *Greek Myths*
Swaddling, *The Ancient Olympic Games*
Burn, *The British Museum Book of Greek and Roman Art*
Cook, *The Elgin Marbles*
Jenkins, *Greek and Roman Life*

Williams, *Greek Vases*
Pearson, *Eyewitness Ancient Greece* (Dorling Kindersley/BMP)

BMES
Ancient Olympic Games pack and video
The Greeks Resource Pack

ASSYRIANS

BMP
Reade, *Assyrian Sculpture*
Tubb, *Eyewitness Bible Lands* (Dorling Kindersley/BMP)

BMES
Assyrian Trails

ANGLO-SAXONS AND VIKINGS

BMP
The Anglo-Saxons Activity Book
Evans, *The Sutton Hoo Ship Burial*
Page, *Norse Myths*
Wilson, *Early Medieval Designs*

BMES
Anglo-Saxon & Viking pack
Sutton Hoo, Saxons videos
The Anglo-Saxons interactive multimedia CDRom (with Research Machines)

ROMAN MOSAICS AND ROMAN SCULPTURE

BMP
The Romans Activity Book
Walker, *Roman Art*
Potter, *Roman Italy*
Burn, *The British Museum Book of Greek and Roman Art*
James, *Eyewitness Ancient Rome* (Dorling Kindersley/BMP)

BMES
Roman Empire pack

OTHER BMES RESOURCES

National Curriculum Art: Key Stages 1, 2 & 3 How the British Museum and the Museum of Mankind can help you
Ankhs and Waterlilies: Teachers' Pack for use with children with learning difficulties

APPENDIX 5

Organisations

Access Committee for England
35 Great Smith Street, London SW1P 3BJ

The Adapt Trust (Access for Disabled People to Arts Premises Today)
Cameron House, Abbey Park Place, Dunfermline, Fife, KY12 7PZ
Tel. 0383 623166

Arts Council
14 Great Peter Street, London SW1P 3NQ
Tel. 071 333 0100

Artsline
5 Crowndale Road, London NW1 1TU

British Council of Organisations of Disabled People (BCODP)
De Bradelei House, Chapel Street, Belper DE56 1AR
Tel. 0773 828182
Minicom 0773 828195

British Dyslexia Association
98 London Road, Reading, Berkshire RG1 5AU
An organisation which campaigns on behalf of people with dyslexia and their families.

The Dyslexia Institute
133 Gresham Road, Staines, Middlesex.
The Institute specialises in tuition, teacher-training and assessment. It has a national network of advice centres.

Minorities Arts Advisory Service (MAAS)
4th floor, 28 Shacklewell Lane, London E8 2EZ

Museums & Galleries Commission
16 Queen Anne's Gate, London SW1H 9AA
Tel. 071 233 4200

Museums & Galleries Disability Association (MAGDA)
c/o The City Art Gallery, Mosley Street, Manchester M2 3JL
Tel. 061 236 5244 ext. 123

National Association of Advisory Officers for Special Education (NAAOSE)
32a Pleasant Valley, Saffron Walden, Essex CB11 4AP

National Association for Special Educational Needs (NASEN)
2 Lichfield Street, Staffs. ST17 4JX

People First (self-advocacy organisation of people with learning difficulties)
Instrument House, 207–215 Kings Cross Road, London WC1 9DB
Tel. 071 713 6400

Special Educational Needs National Advisory Council (SENNAC)
Dept. of Education, The University, PO Box 147, Liverpool L69 3BX.

A fuller list of relevant organisations and individuals is available in the Contacts section of *In Through the Front Door* by Jane Earnscliffe (Arts Council of Great Britain 1992).

APPENDIX 6

Makaton Sign Language

The Makaton vocabulary is an increasingly important element in the teaching of adults and children with learning and communication difficulties in the United Kingdom. It is also used in many other countries including the United States, Australia and Hong Kong. The signs in each case are selected from the sign language of the country, and are adapted to the culture.

Makaton consists of a core vocabulary of 350 concepts and a resource vocabulary of 4000 concepts, selected to suit the needs of the individual child or adult.

The earlier stages of the vocabulary cover very simple concepts and are usually taught first. However, the emphasis of the programme is on personalising the vocabulary to suit the individual need. Some words from the later stages and the resource vocabulary may, therefore, be introduced early on. It enables children and adults with limited ability to master a few signs and/or symbols, thus helping them communicate their basic needs and alleviating frustration.

The Makaton system was originally designed to meet the needs of adults with a learning difficulty and hearing impairment, but its use has broadened over the last twenty years to include a wide range of people with communication difficulties.

We are grateful to the Makaton Vocabulary Development Project for providing us with Makaton symbols for reproduction in this book (1994).

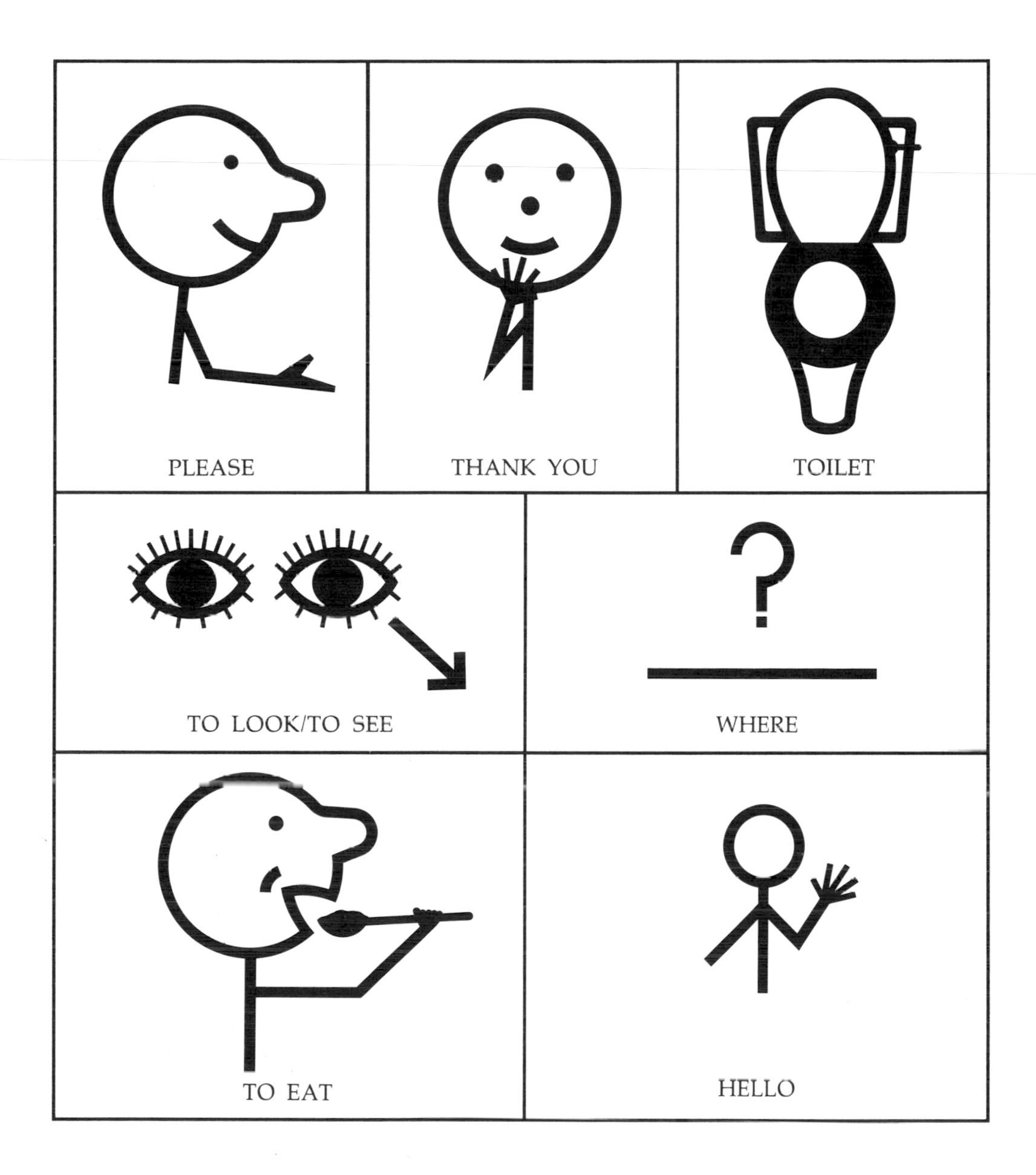

For further information about the Makaton vocabulary, training courses, associated resource materials and the national network of Makaton representatives and co-ordinators, please contact the Makaton Vocabulary Development Project (MVDP), 31 Firwood Drive, Camberley, Surrey GU15 3QD.

Further reading

ARTS AND EDUCATION

Abbs, Peter, *The Symbolic Order*, Falmer Press 1989

Durbin, Gail, Morris, S. and Wilkinson, S., *A Teacher's Guide to Learning from Objects*, English Heritage 1990

Ross, Malcolm, *The Claims of Feeling (Reading in Aesthetic Education)*, Falmer Press 1989

Smith, Edward, *Dictionary of Art*, Thames and Hudson, New York 1984

Taylor, Rod and Andrews, Glennis, *The Arts in the Primary School*, Falmer Press 1993

ARTS AND DISABILITY

The Attenborough Report, Arts and Disabled People, Bedford Square Press for the Carnegie UK Trust, London 1985.

After Attenborough, 1988. Available from: The Carnegie UK Trust, Comely Park House, Dunfermline, Fife KY12 7EJ.

Earnscliffe, Jane, *In Through the Front Door: Disabled People and the Visual Arts, Examples of Good Practice*, The Arts Council of Great Britain 1992

Pearson, Anne, *Arts for Everyone: Guidance on Provision for Disabled People*, Carnegie UK Trust/CEH 1985. Available from: Centre for Accessible Environments (CAE), 60 Gainsford Street, London SE1 2NY.

Arts Council, Arts and Disability Checklist: a quick reference guide for arts officers on arts and disability issues. Arts Council 1989

MUSEUMS

Ambrose, Timothy and Paine, Crispin, *Museum Basics*, ICOM and Routledge, London and New York 1993

Boylan, Patrick (ed.), *Museums 2000: Politics, Professionals and Profit*, Routledge, London and New York 1993

Hooper-Greenhill, Eilean, *Museum and Gallery Education*, Leicester University Press, Leicester 1991

Newbery, Elizabeth, *Collect it: Making Collections – from fossils to fakes*, A&C Black, London 1991

EDUCATION AND SPECIAL NEEDS

Aloysius, Chitra, 'Art Galleries and Special Schools', *Art Education*, April 1993

Ashdown, R., Carpenter, B. and Bovair, K. (eds), *The Curriculum Challenge*, Falmer Press 1991

Daniels, Harry and Ware, Jean (eds), *Special Education Needs and the National Curriculum: the Impact of the Education Reform Act*, Kegan Page/Institute of Education, University of London 1990

The National Curriculum and Special Needs: A Report by HM Inspectorate, HMSO London 1991

The National Curriculum: A Guide for Staff of Museums, Galleries, Historic Houses and Sites, National Curriculum Council 1990

Survey of the use some pupils and children with special educational needs make of museums and historic buildings. Report by HM Inspectors 1988

Disability, Design, Museums, MAGDA (Museums and Galleries Disability Association) 1988

La Fondation de France and ICOM, *Museums without Barriers*, Routledge, London and New York 1991

Illustration acknowledgements

The abbreviation BM indicates that the photo is by courtesy of the Trustees of the British Museum.

p. 17 By permission of the National Gallery, London
p. 24 BM
p. 27 BM G&R 1971.11-1.1
p. 28 BM G&R 1980.10-29.1
p. 29 BM G&R B 299-306
p. 30 BM G&R Sculpture B 287
p. 32 Drawn by Richard Parkinson
p. 33 (*top*) BM EA 1242
p. 33 (*below*) Drawn by Richard Parkinson
p. 34 Drawn by Chitra Aloysius
p. 39 BM G&R 1857.12-20.426 (Cat. of Mosaics 54j)
p. 40 BM G&R Mosaic 29
p. 43 BM
p. 44 BM G&R 1927.2-15.1/EA 847
p. 47 BM 1838.8-19.1 (Cat. of Sculpture 2335, Sarcophagus 1)
p. 48 BM G&R 1805.7-3.33 (Cat. of Sculpture 1685)
p. 49 BM G&R 1805.7-3.44 (Cat. of Sculpture 1746)
p. 50 BM G&R Gem 3577
p. 51 BM WAA 124546
p. 56 BM G&R 1805.7-3.8 (Cat. of Sculpture 2131)
p. 64 Middlesbrough Art Gallery, photo © Middlesbrough Borough Council.
p. 66 Middlesbrough Art Gallery, photo © Middlesbrough Borough Council.
p. 73 From Betty Davidson, *New Dimensions for Traditional Dioramas: Multisensory Additions for Access, Interest and Learning*, Museum of Science, Boston 1991.
p. 80 BM Education Service
p. 91 Makaton Vocabulary Development Project

ILLUSTRATION ACKNOWLEDGEMENTS

The photographs of children on pp 27, 35, 37, 38, 41, 45, 46, 50 and 55 and colour plates 1, 2 and 6 were taken during the British Museum project by Chitra Aloysius, Jenny Wilson and Cheryl Chant.

Front and back cover pictures: Simon Tutty, BM Photo Service.

Colour plates

3 BM WAA 122200
4 BM EA 48001
5 BM G&R 1857.12-20.426 (Cat. of Mosaics 54j)